Dragon insights

Dragon Insights

A simple approach to the I Ching

JILLIAN LAWLER

SIMON & SCHUSTER
AUSTRALIA

DRAGON INSIGHTS
First published in Australia in 2001 by
Simon & Schuster (Australia) Pty Limited
20 Barcoo Street, East Roseville NSW 2069

A Viacom Company
Sydney New York London Toronto Tokyo Singapore

National Library of Australia
Cataloguing-in-Publication data:

    Lawler, Jillian.
    Dragon Insights: A Simple Approach to the I Ching.

    Includes bibliography.
    ISBN 0 7318 0881 9.

    1. Divination - China. 2. Fortune-telling by Chinese characters.
    3. Fortune-telling - China. I. Title.

    799.16

Cover and text design: Greendot Design
Cover image: *Nine Dragons*, China, Southern Song dynasty, dated 1244;
    Chen Rong, Chinese (active first half of the 13th Century)
    Handscroll; ink and touches of red on paper; 46.3 1096.4 cm.
    Francis Gardner Curtis Fund, 17.1697.
    Supplied by the Museum of Fine Arts, Boston.
Set in Adobe Garamond 12pt on 14pt leading
Printed in Australia by Griffin Press

10 9 8 7 6 5 4 3 2 1

Contents

By means of the easy and the simple,
we grasp the laws of the whole world.
When the laws of the whole world are grasped,
therein lies perfection!

Introduction

Dragon Insights are the essence of the *Yi Jing*, or *I Ching*, the Chinese Book of Changes, which has its beginnings and foundation in the teachings and the diagrams by *Fu Xi* (circa 5000BC/2700BC).

People have been consulting oracles in China for thousands of years to obtain advice, guidance and direction in all aspects of life and living. Dragon Insights represent a way to clarify thoughts and give insight into potential deeds and ideas. They show paths and give clues and they never cease to amaze and surprise. The Insights (or Oracles) are not a party game; they are one of your best friends, for through them you can converse with the Dragon that is your inner being or higher consciousness. The Oracles show the perfect way of living to be in harmony with the flow of the Dragon, the *chi* (energy/prana) criss-crossing earth.

What I have endeavoured to do here is distill 23 years of study and research into the simple, everyday form that appears in this book. I followed two Chinese principles to achieve this: the first is that in order to condense or reduce anything, one must first fully expand it. The second principle is that in order to know the future, one must understand the past, the roots and the foundation.

I researched, studied and gleaned knowledge about the *I Ching* and all things Chinese from every available source. (The complete bibliography is longer than this book! An abridged version appears at the back of the book.) I studied Chinese language, astronomy, the weather, and horticultural matters. I then expanded that knowledge into reams of writing, illustrations, charts, and a room full of folders, files and thoughts. I began to condense this vast collection of information and knowledge, and condensed it, and condensed it until it became the dragon's essence – every word chosen for its largeness and visual essence. This book is the essence, the bottom line.

Twenty-three years of experience has taught me that not everybody is interested in how or why the oracles work, or how conclusions were arrived at. A quick, succinct answer to their enquiry is what they want. *Dragon Insights* is for all those people I have encountered since 1975 who want another opinion, or a quick insight into their busy life, or to know if their gut feeling is right, or advice on a situation that has arisen suddenly and must be dealt with quickly. It's also a very good tool for private people who don't wish to share their problems, feelings, ideas and dreams with others. This book takes care of immediate needs and may well get the reader thinking...

I have covered all the realms of life: physical, mental, material, creative, and spiritual, relative to the Oracle. I have answered all the main questions that people have asked over the years, that is, love, money, travel, health, work, study, business, children, homes/houses, and enlightenment.

Even with all my study, it is hard to explain *why* Insights work. I can show you every aspect of how they work and how to work with them, but not *why* they work. I believe it has to do with the 'mathematics of the universe', the movement of the earth around the sun, and the flow of the seasons and nature. Also something to do with human beings being microcosms of the macro-universe – everything occurring outside the body being duplicated inside the body (or perhaps vice-versa).

Since this method of consulting the *I Ching* was first considered in 1989 and the 64 Insights put in a bowl, more than 2,000 enquiries have been made by many different types of people from all walks of life from that same bowl. It is a source of amazement that one Oracle can have so many different meanings according to the question.

Essential information

Fu Xi was the ancient sage who first conceived the concepts and created the foundation of *I Ching* in a diagram that charted seasons and movement, and of him it is said: '*Fu Xi* looked up, he looked down and all around him. He noted the movement of fire (upwards) and water (downwards). He observed the sun's course. He scanned the horizon and scrutinised what was near. He charted the course of the wind and the seasons. He examined seeds and plants and noted their growth, and their flow and movement, the light and shade of yin and yang.' (From *Ta Chuan – the Great Treatise*, Chapter 11 – History of Civilisation.)

This is why the Insights have a 'rural' flavour. They developed from the original Farmering guide devised by *Fu Xi* after he spent all that time observing everything around him. (This developed into the Agricultural or Hsia Calendar 2205–1766BC.) It works on the principle that every seed is an idea, with potential for growth in the field of the mind, the body, the heart and soul. The 'big field' is where one plants these developing ideas so they may grow to abundance and be harvested.

In exactly the same way as a gardener prunes fruit trees, germinates seeds or transplants seedlings only at certain times of the year, the Oracle advises for the doing of the right thing at the right time. It tells us what will benefit our being at a certain time and what will not.

The growing guide This is the sequence of events in the life cycle of a plant, idea, project, endeavour or person.

- The seed germinates, after covering and watering, into a sprout.
- The sprout after nurturing becomes a strong seedling.
- The seedling is transplanted into the field or garden.
- The seedling after nurturing/nourishing becomes a sturdy plant.
- The sturdy plant after nourishing grows to full abundance and sheds seeds to ensure its survival.
- Having reached a state of perfection the plant is harvested.
- Then it is uprooted, pruned back, dies back or it just dies.
- The plant's energy withdraws into the roots or into the soil where the plant's seed waits until the cycle begins again.

Dao

What is Dao? It cannot be seen, it cannot be heard, it cannot be touched, it has no smell or taste. Dao is beyond the senses. *Lao Zi* (circa 500BC), who first voiced the concept of Dao and 'painfully' called it Dao, tells us: 'The Dao that can be expressed is not the eternal Dao. The name that can be named is not the eternal name.' (From Dao de king*)*.

The character for Dao means 'way'; a fixed path, track or course, leading from a beginning directly to the goal. The character was first used to indicate the astronomic course of the stars. The concept of an ever-turning cycle and action in harmony with the seasons and movement of chi.

Chi

The sages of old China defined life as myriad dragon energy channel-lines criss-crossing the universe. This energy that the Chinese call chi is the life essence, the motivating force. It animates all things. It is what the Hindus and the Buddhists call prana; the vital force, the cosmic breath. The concept, direction and flow of chi form the foundation of Chinese sciences ranging from acupuncture, medicine, feng shui, astronomy/astrology and agriculture to martial arts. Chi is what the acupuncturist seeks to activate with the correct placement of needles at certain key points of the body, the acupuncture meridians. The meridians convey life energy, chi, through their own locatable channels within the body. In the same way every structure and space has 'acupuncture' points that harmonise with or obstruct the cosmic flow of energy (chi), the Insights put the enquirer in touch with the chi surrounding the enquiry.

Yin and Yang The Yin and Yang are the basic opposing forces that hold the universe together. The original concepts of Yin and Yang were light and shade. Yin and Yang are always two sides of the same coin.

YANG	YIN
Light	Shade
The sun	The moon
Something shone upon	The cloudy and overcast
Heaven. Masculine. Father	Earth. Feminine. Mother
Positive. Yes. Active	Negative. No. Passive
Creative	Receptive
Proton	Electron
Light. Day. Hot. Summer	Dark. Night. Cold. Winter
Above. Rising. Firm	Below. Sinking. Yielding
On the surface. Fact	Deep or hidden. Intuition
Left side of the brain	Right side of the brain
Right side of the body	Left side of the body

The ancient Agricultural or Hsia Calendar (2205–1766BC) incorporates the movement of the North Star/Orion constellation, using the 'handle' of The Plough or Dipper as the pointer. At nightfall in the northern hemisphere, the handle points to the direction of the current season, that is, spring to the east and autumn to the west; completion of the handle's rotation around the celestial heaven defines the passing of one year. The handle rotates 360 degrees around Tzu Wei, the North Pole Star, approximately every 24 hours.

The use of this book

- **To begin**: Wash your hands.
- Cut out the 64 slips (representing the 64 Insights) on yellow paper, at the back of this book. Fold or roll up each slip of paper individually and place all 64 slips in a bowl or little bag.
- Try to maintain a harmonious, peaceful atmosphere and state of mind while you are preparing the Insights. If you have a special mantra or prayer, then please say this as you work.
- Keep your container and this book together somewhere up higher than your shoulder, or the shoulder of the tallest person in your environment. Ideally, in the southern hemisphere, the place where the Insights are kept should face north and be in a north-west corner. In the northern hemisphere, the place where the Insights are kept should face the south and be in a south-west corner. If you have a shrine or sacred place established, please keep the book and Insights there.

Consulting the Dragon Place your right hand (left hand if you are left-handed) into the bowl or bag, and think about what you would like advice or insight into.

- Swirl/stir your hand through the 64 slips, concentrating on your question.
- Take your time, don't hurry, and try to focus on your question.
- Pull out a slip — note the number and turn to that Oracle/page of the book, putting the slip back into the bowl or bag.

- There is only one answer for each question. Do not ask the same question twice. Why? Because the *I Ching* regards itself as a teacher. A teacher's answer to the question of a pupil should to be accepted as a key for resolution of doubts and a basis for decision. If you keep on asking the same question over and over again without heeding the answer, the teacher (in this case the *I Ching*) becomes annoyed and won't speak to you on that particular matter again.
- You don't have to ask an actual question. It is quite alright to picture the person or thing you are enquiring about in your mind and just keep focus of that picture.
- The use of this book should not be carried to extremes. Before you bought this book you were able to think for yourself so this book should not be relied upon to help you with every single issue that arises in your life. The Insights are about flow, the movement of chi energy along the proper channel at the proper time. An Insight such as number 4, The Fool, or number 47, Exhaustion, will usually tell you if you have asked too many times.
- Do not consult the Dragon when intoxicated. The answers will be erroneous.
- Whether you let other people use your Insights or not is a personal choice. You could ask the insights and find out what they think. I have let many, many people use mine and don't have a problem with it so long as they have not been drinking alcohol on the day.
- The Insights are not set in stone – they are mechanisms of advice. You may follow their advice or not, as you wish.

Interpreting an Insight The Insights are meant to show paths and give clues. They should be not tied down. When you consult the Dragon you are communicating with yourself — with your higher consciousness or inner being, connecting with your soul. You are finding out what your inner being already knows. We human beings only use about 10 per cent of our brains consciously; to consult the Dragon is to tap into the 90 per cent of the brain that isn't consciously utilised.

No single event mentioned in an Insight will apply every single time you draw an Insight. Allow your inner being to transmit its deep, inner images to you and interpret the Insight according to your individual needs and circumstances.

Don't be overwhelmed by words like 'good fortune'. Read the whole Insight carefully. The 'good fortune' will come if the advice offered in the Insight is followed. That which benefits is that which directs the energies toward 'good fortune'.

If you ask the Dragon 'How do I feel or think about something/someone?', the Dragon will tell you your conscious thoughts, not necessarily the truth of the matter. The Dragon will tell you what your conscious mind, the 10 per cent, thinks or has assumed. What you think with your conscious mind may not be the truth of the matter. Better to word the question: 'What is the truth of this person or matter?'

The Layout of each Insight

Each Insight is split into the following sections:

The title character This is a direct translation of the ancient Chinese title of the Insight and has been left floating in its archetypical state to retain the essential essence and image of the original character. As well as the meaning of each character representing the Insight's name, the component characters that go to make up the name character as a whole have been included. Some of them are cute, all of them are thoughtful. Like #20 *Guan*, meaning a view, an observatory or a lookout; the component characters that make up the word *Guan* are person, look, ancient, and beautiful — a person looking at something ancient and beautiful (a view). Contemplate the component characters and the images they convey to you in relationship to your question.

Image The Insights come from a place, space, world, or realm of being beyond our five senses. The image attempts to capture ideas coming into being; beginning to form and develop in the material world of visible things, it endeavours to visualise the original pattern, idea or essence of each Insight. Each image contains an archetypical comment on the Insight based on the visions of King Wen (circa 1126BC – see Insight #36), the diagrams of Fu Xi and occasionally insights gleaned by the author. In ancient texts the reader was encouraged to meditate on these sometimes seemingly obscure images as they contain the germ or seed of the entire Insight and the thought that motivated your enquiry.

Allow your mind to wander freely through the image and contemplate it as you would remember a dream.

In the field glimpses what happened in the farmer's field in ancient times and the growth stage of the crop. Most Insights contain an image of the farmer at work in the field (or not) according to the weather. This word picture should be considered metaphysically or metaphorically in the context of the enquirer's question. The stage of growth and the activities happening in the field equate with the state of growth and activity needed in the matter you have enquired about. Please also read the sections about Fu Xi and The Growing Guide in 'Essential Information'.

A shaman sometimes appears in the field performing rain-making ceremonies. Shaman are the ancient holymen who cured with herbs, prayers and chants, or talismen written in red on yellow paper to repel evil. They used trance to communicate with the ancestors and spirits.

Occasionally mythical, historical or religious figures are mentioned. To find out more about these figures visit the Dragon Insights web site at www.dragoninsights.com or consult the Bibliography at the back of the book and visit a library.

Flow shows the general direction and influences prevalent to the enquiry. Please also read the entry on Chi in 'Essential Information'.

Wealth relates to worldly, spiritual and health wealth, also the qualities that Heaven and the Insight's chi endow you with. This section advises you on worldly wealth and the general action needed to acquire it, but for specifics of worldly wealth, the market-place section should always be considered.

With spiritual wealth, Buddhist as well as Taoist concepts are expressed. Buddhist teachings originate in Sanskrit teachings so some Sanskrit terms occur – such as chakras, the energy centres within the body. For more information on chakras, Buddhism or Taoism, consult the Bibliography and visit your local library or visit the Dragon Insights web site at www.dragoninsights.com

Relationships covers all types of relationships and interactions with all types of people, spirits and occasionally animals.

The Market Place covers the worldly aspects of our everyday life; all the events that occur outside your home environment. This includes all business endeavours, including retail and wholesale buying and selling, shares and futures stockmarket. It also includes career and work opportunities and scholastic achievement.

When something 'benefits' in the market place, it can 'benefit' in many different ways. For instance, in Insight #10, *Lu*, the market place section says, 'The footwear industry benefits.' This means that every aspect and activity connected to the footwear industry is in harmony with the times and will bring good fortune. If you have enquired about career direction or a job, then work in any area of the footwear industry is likely and will be beneficial. If you had enquired about financial investments then the footwear industry or an aspect of it, would be a good investment. If you had enquired about ways to improve your business or add a new product, then introducing a range of footwear may be the way to go. Perhaps it means something as simple as the enquirer or the person enquired about buying or being given some new shoes. It definitely means that all aspects of the footwear industry will prosper.

Travel covers the advisability of travel. Unless the Insight refers to long distance or local travel specifically, then the information applies to any type of travel on your agenda.

Feng shui Mention of feng shui practices, in regards to attaining wealth and success in your goals, appear throughout the insights. A feng shui section appears in some insights.

Feng Shui applies Chinese building, layout, and design techniques and timing to businesses, homes, gardens and farms for an improved flow of energy and the ultimate use of space to increase profit and well-being.

The essence of feng shui is to harmonise the energies of the universe with the activities of the human race. It is the ancient science of positioning everything, everyone and every action in the right place to harmonise, balance and utilise the natural (proper) flow of energy (chi) through everything in the universe. Feng Shui could be considered as the eastern equivalent of environmental studies.

Feng shui is a science, a system, a tool, a strategy; it is not magical; it is essentially based on the movement of the earth around the sun and the moulding forces of wind and water that create the shapes of hills and direction of rivers and water courses. The character for feng means 'wind' and shui is 'water'.

A feng shui practitioner will also be able to provide you with a Chinese astrology chart, or the eight characters for your birthday and show you how to look these up in a

Chinese calendar, as this is also a requirement for success in some Insights.

Miscellaneous information is a mixture of things, little snippets that can't be tied down or sectioned. Many enquirers, depending on their question, find this section the most insightful of all. It sometimes contains little stories about how the Insight unfolded in an enquirer's life. Sometimes it mentions obscure objects or it may be the author's insight into the Insight. Often you find what you are looking for in this section.

1 Qian 乾

Qian means male, creative, heaven. **Qian**'s components are **Qi:** ask alms, beg or pray humbly; **Yi:** a sprout leaving a bud, a symbol of blossoming; **Ri:** sun; **Zao:** early morning; and **Chi:** ten, complete.

Image A majestic midnight blue Dragon, symbolising primal energy and sublime success, rising to the heavens.

In the field The sky over the field is clear and blue. The farmer plants good seed and prays humbly in the early morning sun for a complete or tenfold crop. The seed germinates, becomes a seedling, grows tall and bears an abundance of good fruit, then it is harvested. *Qian* pictures the complete life cycle of a plant, idea or person, from seed to harvesting (see The Growing Guide in 'Essential Information').

Flow *Qian* is complete, positive, yang energy – the Dragon *chi* that causes, creates and pervades the universe. It is primal energy; the inner force that transcends space and time. It is energy from a deep, fundamental core within yourself; total energy that brings creative powers to the fore.

A good idea is the seed and now is the time for planting. You are in the right place at the right time. At first allow your idea or endeavour to develop quietly, until it reaches the 'seedling' stage; a 'see-able' tangible thing.

When faced with choices, try to let your inner self decide the way – go with that gut feeling. Be guided by your personal, ethical and moral sense of things – the standards you believe to be good and true. If you are not swayed by any other standards or opinions, then your influence will spread in a positive and extremely lucky manner.

With success comes the danger of carelessness and arrogance. Beware the ego! Keep your feet firmly on the ground and stay on the side of the ordinary people. Develop sage-like qualities and after the harvest be prepared to make way for a new crop by withdrawing or acting in an advisory capacity. It is a natural law that everything on earth reaches a peak and then begins a decline. Know when and how to stop, and be content. Heaven will bless and reward your actions.

Qian says that if the matter enquired about can be taken through all its transformations of growth, from seed or beginning to success and retirement, then its power, strength or energy will continue to guide or influence events (in its particular field) even though it is no longer visible. It will have set standards and bequeathed an in-depth understanding and order that others will continue to emulate.

Wealth There will be profit and gain on all levels. The physical body is vibrant and strong. Illness will be cured or will go into remission. The primal force, deep within your being, will keep you strong and active.

There is money for the making, and potential for splendid financial growth and prosperity. At the 'seedling', see-able, tangible stage of your endeavour, seek financial aid and it will be available. Everyone's finances will improve but don't be greedy, obsessive or addictive.

At this time, meditation will aid you greatly; a prayer, mantra or affirmation will also benefit you. *Kundalini* energy, rising from the base of the spine, stirs each of the chakras on its journey to the 1,000 petalled lotus at the top of the head.

Relationships Life will be busy, busy, busy! Many people are coming and going, and there is much to be done. All this industrious activity is bound to attract good fortune but it may also attract unwanted attention. Ensure that all dealings with others are ethical on both sides. The subject or object enquired about is an integral part of your essential being; a precious cosmic gift to aid and enhance your journey through life; a good and wondrous thing. Are another person's intentions for the use of your precious gift completely ethical?

At the 'seedling' stage of the endeavour, consult others about its progress and future growth. Your endeavours will meet with encouragement and many people will help. An honourable and influencial person in your field acts as your mentor, and your 'crop' will begin to grow abundantly.

Those that are meant for each other will come together. In love and marriage, everyone is happy. Fertility rates are high. A child enquired about will be an energetic, self-willed, independent, creative, and intelligent deep thinker.

Travel It's a great time for travelling, especially by rail.

Marketplace This is an energetic time in the market place when all business will prosper and grow. An idea or product enquired about has great potential. This is a good time to begin new projects or expand, but keep quiet about your endeavour until it is 'see-able' and tangible. Wait until it is at 'seedling' stage before seeking production aid or financial support. Your career will be brilliant if you follow ethical practices. However, remember the essence of *Qian* is that of a complete cycle, so be prepared and wise enough to withdraw after the harvesting of the 'crop', when your investment or money-making venture has peaked.

Gardeners and farmers can attain abundant crops but may need to install a good irrigation system, as the weather surrounding *Qian* is usually clear and dry.

Feng shui An excellent space for working, creative, active, mentally challenging or motivating processes. *Qian* is an excellent Insight to receive if enquiring about commercial buildings, especially banks, financial houses, the manufacture and sale of jewellery and hardware, management or design studios, or premises for training/fitness, yoga, tai chi, ballet etc. Premises with domed roofs and metal materials such as corrugated iron sheeting, steel girders and metal roofs are especially fortunate. A property enquired about is a great place to make money and/or meditate in, but not good for day-to-day living, resting and sleeping. A good space for a home office or workshop.

Miscellaneous All shades of the colour blue are very significant at this time and may feature strongly in some aspect of your life, dress or decor.

2 *Kun* 坤

Kun means earth, female, receptive. **Kun**'s components are **Tu**
meaning earth and originally drawn to mean a shrine for sacrifices
to the earth; and **Shen**, originally drawn as a bolt of lightning,
meaning the seventh lunar month.

Image A person with a yielding nature experiences supreme
success.

In the field A mother nurtures a child from a baby in the
womb through to adulthood. The farmer makes offerings at the
small shrine in the north-west corner of the field, dedicated to
Mother Earth as the devoted nurturer of all that lives and
moves, constantly providing sustenance and shelter impartially.

Flow Creative, male, yang energy is essential in order to
germinate something but receptive, female, yin energy is
equally important to ensure that which is germinated comes
to fruition and birth. Kun's chi nurtures and protects an existing idea, endeavour or project through all the stages of
growth to successful completion.

Follow along with the flow of things that are going on
around you – don't try to swim against the current or lead the
way. What you are trying to achieve is good and Heaven is
pleased. So let Heaven lead the way and show the path. Use
your intuition – it is clear as a bell at this time. Remain quietly
receptive to the creative impulses flowing from Heaven.

Try to time endeavours so that they will either begin or
come to fruition after the winter solstice.

Wealth Heaven will provide a safe secure environment at this
time, to perfect a wealth-creating endeavour. Wealth comes
about by nurturing an existing idea or endeavour quietly. This
is not the time to start something new, but to work with existing material. Don't look for more work, finish what you
already have to do. Meditation and breathing exercises will

benefit you. Indoor activities will bring prosperity in all realms of your being.

Illness disappears.

Relationships A time of being of service to others. Sometimes this is selfless service without thought of any gains or benefit to yourself.

If you notice that people around you are playing silly, sneaky games, say nothing, but try to work alone. Discretion will win the day. Act behind the scenes, perfecting endeavours quietly before heading for centre stage.

Timing is everything – wait for the right time. If you push ahead by yourself at this time, you will get lost. An honourable and highly placed person in your 'field' sees the light of your shining endeavours and helps you. This will be the time for action. You will obtain a prominent but not independent position. It is not a time to stand as an equal to, and/or opposite to, the leader. You should complement the leader.

There is news from someone who has disappeared.

It is very easy to become pregnant at this time.

Travel Now is not a harmonious time for long-distance travel or even to be generally out and about, unless it is part of your essential daily routine such as going to work, school or shopping.

Marketplace Finally you arrive at a thriving market place with excellent goods or harvest ready to sell. Good fortune is experienced by both the buyer and the seller. A complete cycle has been made, from germination, to harvest, to the market place. A good time for products and articles that are conceived, created, made, and marketed by one person, or one company, or in the same country.

Artisans and writers will make good profits.

Students will pass exams.

Feng shui Repair and prepare your current environments.

Miscellaneous You find what you are seeking. The colour yellow is very significant at this time and may feature strongly in some aspect of your life, dress or decor.

3 Tun 屯

Tun means collect, store up, assemble; hard, difficult; a barracks, a village.

Image Great good fortune in the end if small things are put in order at the beginning.

In the field Small 'sprouts' are growing, seeds are germinating and young things are growing in water. The beginning is difficult. Young things must be tended and nurtured constantly and the field prepared ready for planting out.

Flow *Tun* contains all the chaos, confusion and difficulties that occur when one is trying to bring something new into being. The only way forward is to stop and take time to sort out the tangles one by one and create order. Define what your 'field' is and its boundaries. If venturing into an area of which you have no knowledge, get some help. Stay close to your 'field' and prepare it for the 'seeds' of your endeavours. Once the 'seed' is sown, there will be more difficulties and hard work while you wait for the 'seed' to grow into an abundant crop. Don't lose heart; it is not easy, but objectives can be achieved. Don't let things pile up; attend to all matters as they arise. Gradually your confidence will come and difficulties will disappear. Keep faith – good fortune will come.

Wealth There is not much ready cash about, but things are looking up. New ideas come into being. There is growth on all levels – mental, physical, spiritual, and material. Whatever the state of wealth enquired about, *Tun* says it is just at its beginning – newly born or just about to be. What has been enquired about is going to need a lot of attention and hard work before it grows to full abundance and produces fruit. Right now there is more work, then profit, but be assured that if you can hang in there, a cauldron of knowledge and abundant increase awaits.

An illness is in its early stages. You should seek medical attention and nip the illness in the bud.

Relationships Not the easiest of times for any relationship. Nobody is glowing with confidence. Old or established relationships are sorely tested. Marriage is not very happy. New relationships can be difficult and confusing. People tend to misunderstand each other's intentions and actions.

Whatever you have enquired about, don't push ahead alone; the assistance of others is needed. Wait for an offer of assistance that comes from the right quarter. Don't accept the first or just any offer of assistance. You will make the right connections to gain the assistance needed. Then be cautious, proceed step by step and stay within your limits.

Yes, a woman enquired about is pregnant.

Travel Journeys will not be beneficial. This is not a good time for travel, even though the confusion around may make you think of running away. It is best to stay and see things through. If you must go travelling now, goals can be achieved but there will be many delays and lots of confusion at the beginning.

Marketplace A fairly quiet market place right now. Young and small things will bring profit, large things will not. A new job will be difficult and confusing at the beginning. In business, this is not the time to expand; rather it is time to take care of what is already on your is plate. There is a lot more work to be done getting things ready for market before the profit comes. New business will succeed in time but will require a lot of organisation and capital input to sustain early development. An overdraft, loan or credit facility may be needed.

Any investment in fledgling enterprises or businesses involved with small things or items will reap benefits in the long term, but there will be ups and downs along the way.

Tun talks about entering into a formal regulated agreement or contract with another in order to receive assistance. This contract could take a long time to come to fruition. It could be a deal that is done to ensure survival in the market place until business is well established, or a loan to tide business over until harvest, or perhaps some special equipment or service that is needed. For a student this could be a government HECS loan. This is a contract that not all the parties concerned are happy about. Some people think that the party with whom the contract is made is a rip-off merchant. But those people are wrong; the value of this alliance becomes clear when the contract eventually comes to fruition.

Miscellaneous Marcia received *Tun* in answer to her enquiry about the new job she was starting as office and showroom co-ordinator for her husband. Her husband was a highly successful mastercraftsman, but all other aspects of his business were in a mess.

The chaos, confusion, untangling and sorting out were clearly seen as she collated 652 phone numbers, addresses and bits of customer information, written on scraps of paper or wood, or on the wall, into a database. She discovered the many mysteries of her husband's unique accounting system as she sorted through shoe boxes of paperwork. She created files and order. It took six weeks to sort out her husband's tax matters, but for the first time in 12 years, he received a tax refund.

At the beginning, Marcia found working for her husband was difficult in other ways; territory and boundaries definitely needed to be established as to who was responsible for what. There was more than one heated discussion about respect for each other's spaces and ways of doing things.

The husband also wanted his wife to make sewn items for his showroom. Thus began the quest for the correct sewing equipment. Different offers of assistance came in from various dealers. The first offer was not the best offer. Another manufacturer put them on the right path. During this period, Marcia's marriage was not happy. The husband lacked confidence in her sewing ability. Once the right sewing equipment was installed, Marcia's sewing ability became evident as orders flooded in and she had to hire a helper. Hard work at the beginning of her endeavours definitely paid off for Marcia.

4 Meng 蒙

Meng's basic definition is 'to cheat' or 'wing it', also used in words like 'senseless, unconscious, not clear-headed' and found in words dealing with 'mist'. **Meng** shows a family home with the **Meng** plant growing on its roof. The meng plant is a parasite that grows without roots.

Image Youthful folly. An immature condition. A time of learning and teaching.

In the field The farmer's three exuberant sons indulge in youthful folly. They are young and ignorant. They need guidance and education so they don't grow up to be parasites on society.

Flow Insights give only one answer for each question. If you ask the same question more than once, the Insights will not reply. (See 'How to Use This Book' in the Introduction.) Have you asked this question before? If so, follow the advice given then. If you haven't asked this question before, read on. A learning experience about learning experiences, and the knowledge that such learning experiences are not necessarily all bad or painful. Things may get a little rough, but you will learn and grow from the experience. This is a magical yet exasperating experience. Sometimes you are the ignorant one; looking at the subject of your enquiry from an immature perspective. The subject you are asking about may not even be real, but someone else's fantasy.

Sometimes you are the teacher, and you should keep the message kind, simple and clear. Use discipline but don't shackle exuberant young energy. Ignorant bad behaviour shouldn't be punished by another bad example. For example, a child shouldn't be punished with a spanking for hitting another child, or a student suspended from school for truancy. Whoever the young fool is, eventually they will be capable of thinking, acting and leading intelligently.

Wealth You are looking for all types of wealth in all the wrong places. Find an experienced teacher who uses proper learning methods. Seek instruction in an innocent or childlike manner and good fortune will come.

Little rascals steal money, causing minor losses.

Relationships are not at all what they purport to be. *Meng* pictures one person lusting after another who is rich or powerful or has a nice body, but there is no knowledge of true love or evidence of sincere intent here. There is a lot of sycophantic behaviour going on and everybody is fooling themselves. If enquiring about love and romantic relationships, *Meng* implies that somebody is too immature to love anyone or know what love really is.

Existing relationships can improve if the women involved are treated as equals with equal status, input and respect.

Marriage and partnership may be broken up by a third party.

Babies are born.

Travel If you have already booked the ticket or made plans to go travelling before enquiring of the Insights, then go. You will have a good time most of the time and an interesting time all of the time – but your travels will not be in the least as you imagine they will be. You will learn a lot of things, gain a great deal of confidence and realise what a lot you have to give and teach. However, if travelling is only one of several options at this stage, then consult the Insights again on the other options and activity directions.

Marketplace If enquiring about a new business or investment, this option is not a good idea unless it is an industry related to education. Teachers and students will have good fortune.

Miscellaneous The cosmos does not hold you to account for things done in immature ignorance and which are now deeply regretted.

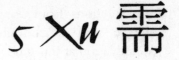

5 Xu 需

The modern meaning of **Xu** is need, want, require, necessaries. **Xu**'s components are **Yu** meaning rain; and **Er,** an ancient character which symbolised a shaman priest. ('Shaman required for rain making.')

Image Rain dragons gather in the sky. Wait confidently assured that a blessing is coming.

In the field Rain is urgently needed for the young crop's survival. The local shaman is performing a rain dance and clouds are gathering overhead. The farmer waits confidently, doing all the little jobs that can be done to make the most of the rainfall when it comes. The rainfall will make it possible for the farmer to achieve great things and an abundant crop.

Flow Whatever has been enquired about, keep the faith as it is going to happen. You can't chase after it but must faithfully wait for it to come (and it will). Then great things are achieved. *Xu* is about waiting for the right time to attempt an endeavour and preparing for it as much as possible. Proceed step by step, not rapidly. *Xu* advises to keep to your everyday ways and routines for as long as possible. Wasting energy in restless anticipation will have detrimental effects later on. If glitches pop up, stay calm and things will go well in the end. Don't waste time laying blame; just fix the problem. Be careful, but unafraid and ambitious.

Wealth Whatever type of wealth enquired about, it is on its way. Prayers are answered. Blessings will come, and success and prosperity are achieved. Try to wait patiently and confidently, and not fall prey to dark brooding. Three unexpected guests arrive – honour them, they are the source of good fortune and wealth. These 'three guests' are usually three actual people, or people with animals, but could also be three good ideas gleaned from listening to another, or three solutions from an unlikely source. Be open to the universe. You will gain money or property.

Meditation at this time will be easy, glorious and fulfilling.

Relationships Treat everyone, including enemies, generously and be kind to strangers. Don't worry about gossip. There is a sense of urgency in the air as you wait for endeavours to materialise and events to happen. It is important to remain cheerful and calm. An opportunity arises to enjoy good food and wine with supportive companions; an opportunity to nourish and revitalise all levels of your being. Make the most of this opportunity; it gives you a more balanced perspective on things and events that are happening.

Quarrels will fade and absent ones will return. Romantic relationships are sincere and wonderful. Those already married are in harmony.

Travel Travel to faraway or remote places brings good fortune.

Don't be put out by delays with travelling – they will ultimately work to the traveller's benefit. All travel will be pleasant.

Marketplace Prepare now for a very busy and lucrative market place very soon. Great things can be achieved but timing is everything, so do not move too soon.

Competition is a good thing right now.

It is a good time for transfers, advancement and promotion.

You get the job and it is a good one.

Miscellaneous A woman who lived in rural Australia, received *Xu* on two different occasions. Once she had been home constantly with a year-old baby and needed time out. That day, three unexpected guests knocked on her door – a girlfriend from town with her young daughter and daughter's friend. They took the baby away and didn't bring him back until the next afternoon. On the other occasion, she asked about rain during a long drought. The following day, out of a clear sky, the 'three friends' arrived — dark clouds, thunder and lightning, then it rained for three days.

6 Song 訟

Song means litigation, contention, bringing a case to court, demanding justice, accusing, disputing, arguing. **Song**'s components are **Yan**: speech, talk; and **Gong**: public, state owned, collective, common, general.

Image Official words – it is best to avoid them. Still at the beginning? Then don't begin at all. Something already begun? Then finish it at the halfway point.

In the field Two people argue. In ancient times, the ordinary people did not like to take a dispute to court. It was only when all other solutions had failed that they took official action, which was very expensive. The accused person was immediately thrown into gaol and even if found innocent, both the accused and the plaintiff were found guilty of disturbing the peace of the locality and the magistrate.

Flow Don't be too confident right now – be wary and apprehensive. If you have projects it is hard to realise them. Do not attempt any great undertakings in any part of your life at this time. Maintain present conditions.

Song talks about disputes, their various stages and how to settle them. When a dispute first begins, try to settle it or drop it there and then. There might be some gossip but don't worry about it.

If a dispute can't be settled immediately because your adversary is in the stronger position and wants to push the dispute on, *Song* says run away, flee, return to the bosom of your family and don't have anything to do with it.

Wealth There really isn't any. You are wrong if you feel that you can gain more, or win outright, by pursuing a dispute to the end – you won't. Compromise – even if you know you are in the right. Now is not the time to push too hard. If there is an opportunity to stop a dispute halfway through its (legal) process, do so. Pushing on to achieve goals through thick and thin and lots of aggravation is not a good idea. Yes, goals will be attained but the battle scars will be many, and any profit or achievement gained will disappear very quickly (within a day/morning).

Don't seek to continue a dispute because your ego has been bruised. Let others take the honours. What goes around, comes around. Nourish the virtues and ideas you know to be good and true. What is an essential part of your being cannot be lost or stolen.

Relationships You encounter crafty, sneaky people. An encounter with criminal law or the police is possible. Be careful of the company you keep, especially if in a new environment.

There is a lot of noise, bravado and ego abounding. However, beating your head against a brick wall will eventually cause you to take thought and consider another direction. You realise the shallowness of what you have been caught up in and find a more enduring course.

Marriages and all types of relationships are very difficult at this time.

Travel Not advisable unless it takes you away from the conflict to a safe, loving environment. If travelling must be done, have plenty of travel insurance and read the details and conditions on it and on your ticket very carefully. Watch out for criminals.

Marketplace Read all the fine print with the strongest magnifying glass available before signing or agreeing to anything. Consider the beginnings of all transactions. Legal hassles could easily develop.

Watch out for shoplifters, pickpockets, robbers, and deceptive business practices.

Definitely do not go into business with a partner.

Miscellaneous If you are asking some specific 'should/shouldn't' type of question; the answer is no, you should not.

7 *Shi* 師

Shi means master, teacher, instructor; a person skilled in a certain profession; an army; a model, an example; to imitate. **Shi**'s components are **Za**: circle or circumference, surround, revolve around; and **Dui**: pile, mass, crowd. People imitate the example of a master; a pivotal leader or a large crowd of people around a central leader.

Image A person receives an unexpected gift, reward, award or commendation in the midst of taking innovative, disciplined action.

In the field A skilled, innovative and well-liked general conducts military training and campaigns with an army of 2,500 men. The general is ready to lead the army into battle. The army is well organised and well trained. The general is well informed about the enemy and full of surprise tactics.

Flow There is opportunity to be had in your field, but success in the endeavour enquired about requires planned, innovative strategies and completely new, fresh tactics. Take a different, unanticipated tack. Don't use the usual pecking order, don't follow the usual route, don't go with the traditional order of things. Give up any preconceived or pre-conditioned outlooks; focus on the object of your endeavour or enquiry, and not the reflections it makes/creates. Try lateral thinking.

These new innovative strategies need to be well-planned and rehearsed before they are used. Military-type order brings success. Be like a general ready to lead an army into battle; as well informed, well trained and organised as possible before proceeding. Then stay in the midst of events; an active participant, directing the movement.

Shi often seems to involve hot, dusty, noisy, exposed, people-filled, public places and locations that drain one's energy. Retreat now and then (take a coffee break) and replenish your energies.

Wealth There is a reservoir of power and strength within you, and a reservoir of wealth around you, with many opportunities for gain on all levels. Such opportunities do not fall into your lap, so go out and actively acquire them with the fresh, innovative strategies described in the flow.

A new meditation technique is not a mistake, but should be practiced in a disciplined, regular way for successful results. Consider the nature of reflections.

Sick people will improve greatly.

Relationships occurring in the time of *Shi* need clear and effective communications. People need to listen, consult each other and practise generosity and fair-mindedness. Try to look at a relationship from a different perspective. Try to find and understand someone's true nature and motives, rather than be swayed by the image they project.

A new partnership of any type will be successful if both parties are flexible and pragmatic; not set in their ways.

An influential person helps you achieve your goal. When success is achieved, employ or use the services of clear-sighted, experienced people, skilled in their field, to maintain what has been gained. Any others who have helped should be sincerely thanked, given excellent references and generously paid off.

Letters arrive from travellers.

Travel should be well organised and informed before departure. Be sure you are looking in the right place for the source of wealth required – you may have things (including the street map) the wrong way around. Travel is noisy, crowded and tiring, but successful. The traveller receives a gift on the journey.

Marketplace There is business rivalry and competition; unanticipated takeovers and manoeuvres. Follow the strategies outlined in the flow and make a surprise attack. Employ a highly experienced innovative person to lead the charge. You will be a winner! Consult with staff or colleagues, implement training schemes, develop a good communication system and well-designed infrastructure or internal systems.

Supplies and resources should be purchased or gleaned from existing stocks that are readily available, stored away somewhere and possibly hidden from view. Don't rely on supplies or resources that are not currently available in stock or yet to be made.

People in areas experiencing drought or water shortage should not rely on expected rainfall. There is an existing water supply to be found. It is underground and hidden from view, most likely in a southern area in the southern hemisphere and a northern area in the northern hemisphere. It is not a silly idea to use a water divining rod to find this cache of water.

Students do well in exams. There is a good energy flow for serious studies, learning or training right now.

Miscellaneous You find what you are looking for.

Isabelle's business was suffering due to cheap, badly made imported copies of her quality, locally made products. She had come up with an idea for a new product but she needed to find the right materials to make it. She consulted the Insights and *Shi* was the answer.

Isabelle followed the advice offered in *Shi*. She devised new tactics, drew fresh strategies, and rehearsed her campaign. she organised herself with a list of possible suppliers, colour samples and measurements. She planned her expedition with her partner as driver.

It was a long day – a very tiring, hard day in hot, noisy city streets and dusty industrial areas. The partner's street directory turned out to be more than ten years old and many of the streets were now intersected by impassible motorways and the like. At one stage, Isabelle realised she was actually holding the map upside down. But Isabelle and her partner persevered and eventually obtained the materials needed. And, as Isabelle was getting out of the car at one of the suppliers, she was rewarded by finding a $50 note lying in the gutter at her feet and so she took her partner to lunch.

8 *Bi* 比

Bi means equalisation, comparison; compare, contrast, collate, classify, sort; each, every, close, near, adjacent; when. The ancient character for **Bi** showed two people, one following another; a union or association.

Image Someone is needed to direct many small streams in order to create a powerful river. Are you the right person?

In the field Two people walk together in the full moonlight, one following another. They have a clear understanding of things; they are not fooled by reflections, they see things as they really are. They follow the law of their inner being and personal ethics rather than what other people say is acceptable.

Flow *Bi* is all about forming a union or partnership with a person or entity. For this partnership to succeed, people must be sure that they are the right person for this union. The enquirer will always be in a subservient but pivotal position, standing next to the leader, holding the group together and bringing a number of different systems together into one sleek central system that covers all, and regulates things. It may be a very pleasant and lucrative position, but it is still a subservient position.

Consider deeply and honestly before accepting this position. *Bi* always involves hard work, often in an environment, which at first has many subtle hostile undercurrents. Are you the type of person who is happy in a subservient position or are you an independently minded person, used to making your own decisions and taking the lead? Consult the Insights again. In a separate question, ask whether your talents, abilities and temperament meet the requirements needed for success in this situation.

If a positive, encouraging reply to that question is received, then get on with it. Don't be late! Don't leave anything to the last moment, or just thinking that all will be well – it won't. If what you have asked about requires physical action, do it straight away.

Wealth is improving and advancing on all levels. There is comfort is your personal life.

Relationships The energy is favourable for love. Those already married or in partnership will prosper.

New partnerships, mergers and alliances will be bountiful if both parties concerned are honourable, truthful, trustworthy and sincere people. If you are sure you know where the other person is coming from and what their intentions and agenda are, you have success. Be objective, not subjective, about this union. *Bi* says associations should be based on truth. Hold on to what you believe in with sincerity and confidence; believe in the strength you carry within. Don't act in a sycophantic manner. Maintain friendly acquaintance with everyone, but avoid close association with negative or petty-minded people as this stops those who can aid your endeavours from approaching. When the right association is formed, be open, forthright, and supportive about it. If you go on hesitating to commit yourself openly to the relationship, you will be left alone.

When obstacles and unobliging people are encountered, just keep smiling and get on with the job. Gradually the hostile undercurrents will disappear.

Travel Observe the moon in the night sky, from a mountain high above the plains. Travel is wonderful and illuminating if you are sure of your direction. Try to organise yourself well in advance.

Marketplace Business and career are both in a good position to prosper – not market leaders yet, but making an impact nevertheless. Try to streamline your business or enterprise into a more sleek, centralised entity. Try to think of ways to reduce paperwork and improve communications.

The student receives a degree.

Miscellaneous You find what you are looking for.

9 Xiao Chu 小畜

Xiao means small. **Chu** means feed, nourish, domesticate domestic animals; keep in store, raise, rear, restraint; retain, reserve, leave behind. **Chu's** component characters are **Tian**: field; and **Xuan**: purple, profound, mysterious.

Image Preparing and waiting for something that is not going to arrive or happen as soon as you would like it to.

In the field The farmer prepares all the seedlings ready for the rain that is expected at this time. But the rain does not come. The wind gathers clouds in the sky, but still it does not rain. Then the farmer makes an offering to the spirits of the ancestors and prays that the rain will come soon. But still it does not rain. Eventually it will rain but the farmer cannot make it happen; he must wait for the rain to fall naturally.

Flow Preparing for success. Things are still in a preparatory state; great things cannot be achieved just yet. It's time for doing the many small things and tasks that, added together, make a big achievement.

Xiao Chu says to return to the courses of action that are either easy and natural for you, or expected of you due to present circumstances and commitments. This opens up current options considerably. Don't be stubborn, be patient. Pushing on before the time is right leads to hindrances, hassles, arguments and accidents. Advancement may look easy at the moment, but it isn't.

Get on with everyday routine matters. Allow things to happen at the proper time; don't try to force growth. It is going to rain, but you cannot make it happen; you must wait for the rain to fall naturally. Now is the time to prepare and make ready. Use all your mental, physical and material skills to prepare yourself for extremely fortunate results at a later date.

Wealth There isn't a lot of money around right now — draw on your resources. Wealth will come with the completion of the matters worked on. Small things and actions succeed on all levels. Buying, selling, making, fixing and taking care of small things brings prosperity in all realms of your being.

A feng shui plan brings good fortune as it will deflect a lot of the negative influences prevalent in your environment at this time.

The greatest wealth is found in the people that surround you at this time – you are a source of admiration and reliability for them.

Your inner nature can be further refined and developed with yogic or Daoist breathing exercises.

Relationships Keep tyrannical people and people with dubious habits under control with friendly persuasion and gentleness, until the time comes when there is enough strength and power available to remove them. It is a time of influencing in a positive way those things, people and events whose essential natures cannot be permanently changed.

Sharing with neighbours and friends is good. When the time is right, join together with neighbours; combining resources doubles strength and power. A good time for a small dinner party.

In love and romance, troubles and suspicions are mainly stress-related and will pass. Partners need to speak openly and honestly with each other.

Travel It is not a good time to go travelling.

Marketplace Business is quiet with some confusion and difficulty at first, then success will come. It is a good time for the development of new ideas or goods.

In farming districts, crops may be affected by drought or insufficient rainfall. Not a good time to speculate in the crop-futures stockmarket.

Sales, advertising, graphics, and electronics benefit.

Miscellaneous If you are waiting for someone or something to arrive, it won't happen today.

10 Lu 履

Lu means shoe, footstep, walk, tread, honour, fulfil, perform. It is found in characters denoting the beginning or first of something. This may have something to do with the *Ching Ming* (pure brightness), a festival which in very ancient times began as a spring holiday called 'Treading the Green Grass'.

Image A person succeeds brilliantly at something risky or dangerous by using good manners and a gentle approach.

In the field Somebody steps on the tail of a tiger and the tiger does not bite them. Such good fortune! There are hazardous conditions ahead. Brave, quick action is successful.

Flow Who or what is the 'tiger'? It could be an aggressive person you encounter. It could be the enquirer in a very angry mood about a presumed injustice. It could be a person born in the year of the Tiger or a place with Tiger in its name. Depending on the question asked, this tiger could also be an establishment or entity that perceives you as a threat, or that you perceive as a threat. In either case, both parties are wrong; good fortune will come of an alliance formed between yourself and this establishment or entity.

You succeed at a dangerous enterprise with inner power and outward caution working together. This is not the time to rush and be careless. Plan your moves carefully before acting. Then advance resolutely. Keep your moves simple, modest and reserved, to avoid conflict or legal entanglements.

Meet unexpected events with equilibrium. These events are not of your own doing or making; they will arise and pass away like a scene from a movie.

There is a difference between bravery and foolishness. Pushing onwards recklessly and against all odds should only be attempted if the matter enquired about is part of one's primal being and essential nature.

Wealth If what you have been doing is to the good, karmicly speaking, then your karma will keep you safe and be your fortune. Enterprises will end well and bring happiness.

The phoenix sings. Sages and saints are born. Illness disappears.

Relationships When dealing with irritable, rude people (and there are a few of them about in *Lu*), the following words and phrases are a vital life lesson not to be forgotten: pleasant manners, care, concern, kind, gentle, smiling, gracious, sympathetic, a lovely soft voice, and looking beyond outward appearance. A smile and gentleness win the day. This formula will make things better, no matter how horrible the person may be.

Long-awaited travellers bring news.

Travel will provide exciting times and bring unexpected profit, but staying in a secluded environment instead of going travelling also brings success. Delays when travelling will benefit the traveller.

Marketplace There will be success in business.

A business or enterprise that can provide really excellent customer service at this time will ensure its ongoing success in the market place and reap vast profits. Remember, excellent customer service is not just a pleasant person on the end of a phone. It is the ability to have swift solutions and tangible back-up for unhappy customers.

The stockmarket's share prices fall and rise sharply and suddenly.

The footwear industry benefits.

Something that is a bit of a gamble or is not a solid secure investment – perhaps an adventurous investment – pays off.

It is not too late to begin a new venture. Enterprises begun at this time will endure successfully for a very long time.

Scholars will rejoice.

There is still time to plant a new crop successfully.

11 Tai 泰

Tai means safe, peaceful; great, extensive, grand, excellent, superior, liberal, broadminded. **Tai's** component are **Shui**, meaning water and **San**, meaning three, depicting in this instance the harmony between the great powers of Heaven, earth and humankind.

Image Yin and yang are in perfect harmony. This brings prosperity and occasions for joy.

In the field *Tai* depicts a large amount of water flowing in a stream. It pictures the time after the harsh winters of China when snow and ice are melting, water is moving again, and the earth is soft enough to plough. The farmer is labouring in the field beneath heaven, sky and sun. Everywhere, fresh-looking tender young things are popping up. The farmer is happy and hopeful as the crop is planted out.

Flow The harmonious balanced chi of *Tai* carries prosperity and good fortune. Humility, activity and hard work bring success. You are in the right place at the right time. There are genuine good guys in control and social harmony prevails. It is a time for the noble and the great; a time of service and benefit, bringing blessings to all.

An original idea, endeavour or project is now tangible, 'see-able'. It's time for transplanting into your 'Big Field', but there is a huge amount of work to do in preparing the 'field' and even more to learn. Taking it easy is of no benefit.

Your 'field', just like the farmer's field, must be defined, contained, ploughed, fertilised, and irrigated.

At such a fruitful harmonious time, the dangers of decadence, sloth and greed are ever-present. Don't be too smart or pushy. Lead at this time through example and action; give and receive hands-on experience. Note all the small things around you, and nurture or uproot them accordingly.

There is a tendency at this time to reverse oneself and

change the direction currently being taken. Keep on your present path but easy does it – your endeavours are not really as far advanced as you may think.

Wealth The harmonious chi of *Tai* makes all aspects and types of wealth blossom and grow. Prospects are excellent and gradually your flow of wealth will increase.

A supply of the type of wealth required is available; you just have to tap into it (like an irrigation system that takes water from a river and spreads it where required for the crop in the field). So you need to create channels and inlets. For example, on a business or monetary level, irrigation equates with cash flow and could relate to something as simple as attaching an overdraft facility to a bank account so that money is available when needed to 'water' the business. Whatever the type of wealth required, you will find assistance. Don't be afraid to ask.

Relationships There is harmony between Heaven, earth and all living beings. All types of relationships are fruitful and balanced. Partners on all levels and in all realms complement each other. Romantic prospects are excellent.

The yang male creative energy of the sun warms the yin female earth. Yang creates movement; awakening the receptive life in the earth and fertilising it. Yin and yang energy come together and for one wondrous, cosmic moment they are in perfect balance. There is a pleasant and harmonious interaction between the two polarities. The mother and father are in harmony. It is a good time for conceiving. Those who endeavour to make peace between opposing groups or individuals will succeed.

Travel *Tai's* flow of energy makes travel for business or pleasure a very pleasant option. Not only will travel be hassle-free, it will add honour and distinction to your reputation and give a balanced viewpoint. But once the journey has begun, it is best not to change its direction.

Marketplace The market place is a pleasant and lucrative place to be, with many opportunities for advancement. All business makes progress and gains.

Innovative ideas and young or new things promise success.

Childcare centres, for 0–3 year olds, benefit.

Plant nurseries benefit.

The employed have opportunities for promotion and achievement.

The unemployed find work in a pleasant environment.

Students pass important exams.

Miscellaneous You find what you are looking for.

An author sent off what she thought was a finished manuscript to her publisher. She had worked long and hard to hone and complete the book and was feeling pleased with herself. She consulted the Insights to see what they thought of the manuscript and *Tai* was the answer.

On the one hand, our author was very pleased to draw such a positive and fortunate Insight as *Tai*; on the other hand she was startled by the parts of the Insight that said there was still more work to be done preparing and defining her 'field' (that is, her manuscript) and that her endeavours were not as far advanced as she thought. Our author decided those parts of the Insight mustn't apply to her in the context of her question and was positive that her publisher would be delighted with her efforts. A couple of days later her publisher rang to say that they were pleased with the manuscript and were accepting it, but it still needed a lot more work in certain areas.

Our author at this time was also experiencing a slight cash flow problem. But she didn't think she was due any more money from the publisher until the book was published. About one month later, during the course of a conversation with her publisher, she discovered that she should have been paid a fee for delivering the manuscript and the publisher had not notified the accounts department about it. So if she had asked for money as *Tai* suggests, she would have received it.

12 Pi 否

Pi means denying, refusing, declining, no, not, never, neither, bad, wicked, evil. **Pi's** component characters are **Bu**: no, not; and **Kou**: mouth, opening, entrance. **Kou** is used in characters concerned with communications and entry points.

Image No entry. Not open. The closing of the gates. No communication. Declining activity.

In the field Standstill and stagnation are close at hand. The autumn equinox occurs when, as at the spring equinox, the weather is equitable and there is a balance of daylight and darkness. However, unlike the spring equinox when summer was on its way bringing warmth and abundant crops, the autumn equinox heralds winter — cold and darkness. Autumnal decay is setting in; the earth will become passive again. The wise farmer realises that it is time to begin withdrawing from active work in his field. After the field has been harvested of its present crop and tidied up, it won't be replanted at this time but allowed to lay fallow until the spring. The soil needs this time to restore its energy and nutriments before it can successfully produce another crop.

Flow For one perfect moment, summer's creative, male, yang energy and winter's receptive, female, yin energy are in harmony before moving off in opposite directions. People are advised to follow the wise farmer's lead and not participate in new activities in their 'field'. Things may look equitable right now but a wintry time is nearing. It will get darker and colder. Avoid hasty actions.

The influence of people of worth (including you) is on the wane. The influence of opportunistic pretenders is on the rise. Your good influences, activities or assets are not valued at this time. Some of your associates may be in the same situation. It is best to withdraw from the situation with these like-minded people. Right now is not the time to go forwards actively asserting oneself; now is the time to find a safe, warm place and close the door. Your time is best spent strengthening and renewing internal energy sources and honing skills and knowledge. The channelling of all your energies and abilities in one direction will be beneficial.

This state of events is a natural occurrence in the cycle of time and will pass. Just as winter cannot be stopped, the advance of negative forces cannot be stopped at this time, but just like winter, they will disappear again when the spring comes. The pretenders who come to power during this time are secretly ashamed of their inadequate abilities.

Observe your 'field' and don't be afraid to go forward when conditions and energies change and new opportunities arise again. But just as the farmer will have to prepare the field again after winter, you will also have to be active and industrious in overcoming the stagnation.

Wealth There are many devious people about. It would not be wise to participate in public activities where these tricky people are involved, even for astronomical amounts of money. Do not seek honour and fame at this time. Do not accept money that you have not worked for or earned. Beware of moneylenders and high interest rates to see you through the rigours of a lean, wintry time.

All types of wealth are hard to come by right now and money may be a source of concern. But because you are prepared to stick to your ethics, principles and values, Heaven will see you through. There will be progress and rewards later on. To give and receive kindness, charity and aid is the right action to take at this time.

Meditation and exploration of your relationship with your inner self or higher consciousness will bring contentment and growth. Now is the time to achieve a spiritual milestone or goal.

Relationships Long and old friendships bring benefits. New partnerships of any kind should be put on hold while one explores the situation further. There is a strong possibility that although the intended partner and yourself are now looking at things from the same perspective, if either one of you makes a move to extend yourselves, your projected paths and opinions will differ and take opposite directions.

Marriages experience difficulty.

Travel Travelling is not advised at this time unless it is taking you to a safe, warm place of retreat.

Marketplace In business or corporate spheres, it is not the time for an honest trader to be doing deals — things are not what they seem. If you must sell, sell now before there is a drop in price or wait until the 'spring', when the cycles moves on and conditions change again for the better. Interest rates will rise. Now it is not a good time for career advancement. Employment is hard to find. However, it is a good time for study.

All textile industries benefit.

Charitable or welfare organisations receive a boost in donations, goods and/or help from volunteers.

Second-hand clothing stores thrive.

Miscellaneous It was late summer when Marie received *Pi* in answer to a question about her job that she had more or less already made up her mind to leave. She didn't like the new store policies, the reduction of staff, and the cost cutting. The new store owner called it economic rationalism, but Marie called it greed as the store always made excellent profits. When she handed in her resignation, her boss offered her bonuses and more money to stay, but she knew in her bones that it was time to go. She enrolled in some business courses. The part about textiles in the 'Marketplace' gave her some good money-making ideas because she could sew. She supported herself by making a range of soft furnishings. Money was tight, but there was always just enough including the money she kept finding because she walked everywhere. Marie finished her studies and after much hard work she now has her own store with people sewing for her.

13 *Tong Ren* 同人

The characters **Tong Ren** together mean men of the same class, colleagues or partners. **Tong** means same, equal, similar, identical; all united, in harmony, in common, in company with. **Ren** means man or human being.

Image A great undertaking is achieved when people unite openly with their peers.

In the field A group of people, all more or less in the same situation and of equal status, meet together to discuss edicts issued by a ruler and/or achieve a mutual goal.

Flow *Tong Ren* is all about participating as part of a group. There are some internal disagreements about the best way to achieve the group's aims. There are noisy meetings; with many people loudly debating issues and tactics, people laughing, people being told to settle down and listen to the speakers. Some members are not as open as they should be and secret meetings occur between various factions of the group. Some members of the group hide their talent, knowledge and ideas until they are sure it is a good time to display them. Other people are busy making contingency plans (business or personal) and working out tactics to be used should a particular situation arise. Yet another faction of the group are ready to defend the traditional ways of doing things. There are secret encounters and communications about the use of entrances and openings. But then there is a reconciliation with more laughing, crying and debating – and finally success and agreement. The ideal goal of equality and the union of all mankind might not be achieved but the current situation is radically improved.

Wealth All types of wealth are waiting to be collected. All you have to do is actively set about collecting it. Be open and vocal about your objectives; you have the clarity and strength to achieve them. Someone aids you about the direction your wealth collection should take. This person could be a mythical, religious or ancient historical figure, or a clairvoyant.

A feng shui plan of the environment you are collecting wealth in would be a great aid to you as this wealth involves organisation and putting everything in its proper place.

A new commitment you may be contemplating brings gains and is not a mistake.

Relationships Go outside your circle of family and friends to find success. Go out there with an impartial, open mind, and talk with as many different kinds of people as possible (whatever their colour, creed, sex or sexual persuasion).

A group of people are living or working together for the same end. Members of this group should avoid conflict, have patience, and each do their share of the duties involved.

Tong Ren says that for a succesful union of people there needs to be at least one conciliatory, yin-type personality amid a group of strong-minded individuals.

When two people are as one in their hearts, nothing can stop their union.

There is success in marriage. All goes well with all types of partners.

Missing people are seen again. The traveller arrives.

Travel is favoured. All roads are open to the traveller.

Marketplace Unions, cooperatives, conventions, seminars and meetings are all in the limelight. This is good news for the people and industries that service such events.

Talks and meetings held at this time should be frank and honest. Everyone involved, no matter how remotely, should be able to participate in this meeting. The venue for this meeting should be such that all concerned parties can see and hear. This may require TV, video conferencing, Internet and the use of digital technology.

There are good prospects for a career involving speaking. The person enquired about, or the enquirer, has the capacity for leadership and the ability to organise business, political parties and groups.

In business generally, initial obstructions in a new venture will be removed by the actions of leaders or authorities. There will be competition and some hair-raising moments, but success in the end. At first the profits are small but they will increase. Afterwards, business is smooth.

There is great success for markets especially open-air markets and food vendors.

Miscellaneous A very worried mother received *Tong Ren* when enquiring about her 20-year-old son who had left his live-in job in the countryside without telling her and she didn't know where he was. Later that week, the son phoned his mother. He was back in the city and had moved into a small flat (comprising one bedroom, one everything else room and a tiny bathroom) with another seven young men. Their combined objective was to pay as little rent as possible so that they could save money for more travelling. These young men slept all over the flat, on the sofas (which they got off the street) and the floor. This was a fellowship of men with all the raucousness described in the 'Flow'. It was noisy. There were arguments, debates and jokes. Chaos and uncleanliness seemed to reign. They were always arguing about the use of entrances – who had the key, who left the door open all night, who deadlocked it before leaving for work with the only key in his pocket and left everyone else inside unable to leave, who came through it for a visit and who else was allowed to stay. But the plan paid off and the young men acquired enough money to buy a van and they travelled together up the coast.

14 Da You 大有

The characters **Da You** together mean Great Possession. **Da** means great. **You** means having, possessing, abundance, plenty.

Image Having greatness. Count your blessings, for they are many.

In the field The sun shines in the sky. The farmer has a Great Possession – an abundant crop just harvested. The farmer is taking his Great Possession to the most suitable market place. Along the way the farmer must keep the crop hidden from robbers. There is transport (a big strong wagon) available, capable helpers to assist the farmer, and enough strength to carry the Great Possession to this place. There, the farmer can meet with others who also have Great Possessions and exchanges can be made with sincerity and confidence.

Flow It is a time of great wealth in all the realms of your being. Your light and clarity grows bright and strong. There will be supreme success in your endeavours.

The time of Great Possessions is not an easy time. *Da You* advises on dealing with this Great Possession, so that you are not overwhelmed by it. Whether an inner wealth or material wealth, if the Great Possession is displayed openly, it will attract negative influences that will hamper endeavours to use it as it should be used. In the beginning, *Da You* advises caution; if matters are managed simply and the Great Possession is not displayed openly, a wondrous period of creativity, knowledge and light comes about.

Maintain humility, modesty and honour.

Wealth There is a wealth of knowledge inside yourself that perhaps you never realised existed before, even though you were born with it. You will enjoy wealth of all kinds in profusion – spiritual power, but also abundance and material prosperity. Make sure this wealth is shared with others.

Make a donation; a gift from the Great Possession of cash, goods or services; give to charities and people in need. In ancient times the gift was given to the Emperor at the Palace. Perhaps part of your donation should go to the 'Emperor' at your own 'Palace'.

In meditation, you will be able to tap into inner primal energy and feelings. The Ajna Chakra, the third eye, and the spiritual heart chakra are connected and operating.

Unfortunately, if you have enquired about sickness, this is also in abundance. Seek medical treatment.

Relationships *Da You* says to keep your ego and pride, inflated by the Great Possession, under control; and resist the temptation to use the Great Possession to compete with others for position and honours.

Wise people and sages are seen. Things are fine for all types of partnerships. The person you hope to see is not far away.

Travel Your goal will be achieved by going to a place to the south in the northern hemisphere, or, to the north in the southern hemisphere. Dignity and humility will win the day.

Marketplace With this abundantly wealthy energy pervading the market place, it is naturally a lucrative place to be. Use caution at the beginning of an enterprise. Be sure of patents, rights, royalties and agreements before putting a product into the market place.

Keep displays simple.

There are many opportunities and options available to you in business, career or academic activities, so choose thoughtfully.

The transport industry benefits.

You benefit the most from this energy by seeking or starting work or business in another place or position (see 'Travel').

You are well appreciated at your workplace and will make advancements.

Miscellaneous Nourish yourself for a great undertaking in the future.

15 Qian 乾

Qian means humility, modesty. **Qian's** component characters are **Yan**: speech, word, and **Jian**: double, twice, simultaneously, concurrently, together with equality.

Image Modestly a person carries out their endeavours and finds happiness.

In the field Two people speak together with equality. They find treasure in the field and share it equally; reducing that which is too much, increasing that which is too small. Balancing and equalising are the key words.

Flow The endeavours enquired about are suppose to be done. They will be accomplished by working late into the night. Heaven ensures that the energy needed to fulfil this agenda is available, successfully bringing 'things' to a conclusion. No fanfare, no special effects; just getting things done quietly, almost secretly. Don't waste energy and time talking about what is being done, just DO it. *Qian* is about working to accomplish the goal or project. While working on these endeavours, you need to keep up encounters with the everyday masses, as it is through these interactions that you are assisted in various ways to complete the special endeavour.

North-west in the southern hemisphere, or south-west in the northern hemisphere, is the direction in which to head for success. This is a literal direction, so check the street directory or map and see where this exact direction leads to from your current living or working environment.

Wealth *Qian* isn't about instant wealth and fame; it is better than that because Heaven supports your path and ensures that everything arrives as it is required, in all realms of your being.

Relationships It is a time to be part of the crowd of everyday, hard-working people. Live humbly and simply on an equal par with the general masses. Behaving in this way will bring about massive relief from inner tension.

Any type of partnership or union formed at this time will be happy and successful. Partners suit each other well. They find 'treasure' in each other. This harmony and 'intuneness' with each other enables them to work and function well together to the same end; leading to the making and finding of 'treasure' in the material world.

Men get along well with women. The husband should listen to his wife's ideas.

A woman manages a household and/or business competently.

Qian also stresses that humility is not about being a doormat for other people.

Equality is *Qian's* message.

Quarrels and illness are rare.

Travel Journeys for business, study or creative purposes bring good fortune. Lost travellers return home.

Marketplace There is an excellent market place for your product, enterprise or activity in an area or suburb to the north-west of your present location in the southern hemisphere or a south-west direction in the northern hemisphere.

Look at your business and note what there is too much of and try to think of ways to reduce it. Is someone doing too much work and another person not doing enough? Are some of the products too big or too small? Is one part of the endeavour demanding too much attention while another equally viable part is not getting enough attention? This is a time to balance and equalise all facets of your business by working hard, late, and long.

The *Qian* market place is best for quality products and enterprises that are accessible to everyday people. Products and services aimed at the extreme ends of the market are either too expensive or too cheap and do not benefit.

There is success for writers in book or article form.

It is a good time for industries involved with weights, measures, and balances.

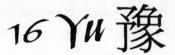

16 Yu 豫

The character **Yu** means prepared, prearranged, beforehand; easy, peaceful, happy, satisfied. **Yu**'s components are **Xiang**: appearance, shape, image; imitation, resemblance, phenomenon; elephant; and **Yu**: give, bestow.

Image To give or bestow shape and appearance on something. Preparing to perform. Prearranged action. Music and dance.

In the field Soon it will rain and strong seedlings can be transplanted into the paddy field. Everything must be made ready for the rain's arrival. The field must be thoroughly prepared. The farmer has workers standing by ready to start planting as soon as the rainfall fills the paddy. The farmer ensures that everybody knows the role they are to perform and what is expected of them.

Flow Vibrant energy and enthusiasm fill the air. Have complete confidence – the action now being taken is right. There will be happiness and good fortune for those who are prepared. Long-awaited results and outcomes are imminent. A prolonged state of tension is about to go; relief is close at hand. This state of affairs makes people very excited and enthusiastic.

Enthusiasm should be controlled at the beginning of an endeavour. Over-enthusiasm drains the chi, leaving little energy to actually get on with the task that you were so enthusiastic about in the first place.

Enthusiasm should unfold in pre-arranged easy actions, in flowing motions that use energy and movement in a controlled manner. Be ready to move and perform when the right moment arrives, just as a musician does not wait until the moment of a major performance before planning and rehearsing the music to be played. The musician would have selected music, considered sound systems, choreography, lighting, props, equipment, and all the other things needed for the best performance possible.

Wealth You are the source of enthusiasm and happiness, and achieve great things and receive great gains. New undertakings will bring good fortune. Everything needed for advancement should be made ready. You should mobilise your helpers and 'troops' into action. Lateral thinking will be beneficial.

It is a good time for any religious undertakings.

Relationships Many friends and acquaintances gather around you, buoyed by your enthusiasm and confidence. Get on with things, don't waste time and energy talking about it. You might be talking to the wrong people; people who do not have your best interests at heart.

Honour your ancestors with candles, incense, flowers, food, drink and music.

There are no obstacles of any kind to marriage or unions and partnerships. Nor will there be any difficulty in reaching an agreement with third parties.

Travel Journeys are fortunate. Take care on the roads. Travellers who have been away return.

Marketplace Prepare your business or endeavours for a great opportunity.

The direction of your career is assured.

Students pass exams, scholars gain honours.

It is an excellent time for the theatre and entertainment businesses; for anyone involved in song, dance, music or pantomime. The singing and dancing *Yu* talks about is not free-form dance or a musical jam session but choreographed dance movements to pre-arranged music.

Ensure that adequate security systems are in place and in good working order.

17 *Sui* 隨

Sui means follow, come or go along with, comply with, adapt to. Its components are **Fu**: a mound or small hill; fat, fertile, abundant, rich; the **162nd** radical meaning halt, found in characters pertaining to movement, journeying, arriving and concepts of distance; **Zuo**: left side, the left; **Gong**: work, job, skilled labour, service; and **Yue**: moon, lunar month, month.

Image Following the course of the day and being of service to others now, in order to rule later on, has supreme success.
In the field Seedlings have been transplanted into the field. This crop will develop gradually from spring to autumn. In order to achieve an abundant crop and wealth, the farmer must tend the crop each day, from sunrise to sunset, going step by step, doing each routine job at the right stage; being constantly active. From morning till night, weeding, hoeing, maintaining, and irrigating must be done. After the crop is harvested and marketed, the farmer will have time for other interests.
Flow Daylight occupations and activities. At nightfall, relax, rest and recuperate quietly in your home. Conserve your energy – too much excitement isn't good. Unlike #15 *Qian*, which advises working late into the night and missing sleep for awhile, *Sui* advises getting on with daylight activities and having regular hours for rest.

In all things do not lose heart – you are in a beneficial position. Plans will meet with success. Go out and communicate with those concerned. Keep to accepted manners, forms, and ways; it is not a time to rock the boat.
Wealth steadily increases on all levels with regular activity. *Sui* heralds the beginning of a cycle of service, working for other people and/or for the benefit of other people's dreams and goals, instead of working on your own projects and goals. Learn to adapt to this routine situation; welcome it as

a gift from the universe. Don't waste time with mistaken resistance. The time of *Sui* broadens your understanding of your personal goal. It increases your confidence in yourself. It gives you the experience and insights needed to make the achievements of your personal goal much easier. *Sui* is actually a step along the way to your goal. Service to others is now the road to freedom with a whole new set of options and the lifestyle of your choice later. Commitment to achieving something 'good and beautiful' brings good fortune in the future and the thought of it brings joyful movement now.

Illness disappears without the help of medicine.

Relationships Keeping company with shallow-minded people, and trying to follow people of intellectual power at the same time, cannot be done.

Marriage is good.

Quarrels are over.

A kind, considerate and generous older man wins the admiration and love of a young woman.

Travel will be alright if you stay on, or close to, the beaten track. Daylight travel is favoured. Heavy loads can be transported. Distant regions can be reached.

Marketplace This is not the right time to begin a 24-hour per day business or commit yourself to extra work or a second job in the evenings. The nine-to-five day job or activity is the way to go at this time for fortunate outcomes later. Daytime businesses and endeavours fare very well.

Labour-saving devices are helpful and beneficial.

The transport/carrier/courier industry benefits.

Students will find good jobs.

There are promotions for working people.

The unemployed will find a day job that they like.

18 Gu

The character **Gu** means poison, destruction, a legendary venomous insect. **Gu**'s components are **Chong**: insect or worm, and **Min**: vessel or container. Insects in a container. In ancient times, shamen used the poison of the insect named **Gu** as a magical potion and as medicine.

Image Matters of correction bring huge and far-reaching changes, and supreme success.

In the field The farmer feels sluggish, dull-witted and defeated. Many essential jobs around the farm have been neglected. The farmer has followed the wrong advice about crop layout in the field. Now the farmer has rotting and stunted crops, sour soil and general land degradation. This can all be fixed but the farmer will have to start all over again from the beginning, removing or fixing everything that has been corrupted before reformation and renewal can occur. This is like pushing a millstone up a hill – it requires major effort.

Flow A time of putting society in order and fixing or repairing 'things' that have been neglected. Afterwards there is order. In this situation, 'things' have been swept under the carpet for a long time. Now the carpet must be lifted and the decaying matter underneath cleaned out properly. Energy and decisiveness must replace dull-minded sluggishness. You should try to brighten your attitude, lose bad habits and energise yourself.

Wealth You have been working with incorrect information. Conditions may be bad now but improvement is possible. Things can be changed, and new beginnings created, with able helpers. Repair brings renewal and prosperity.

Before starting on your new course to fix the decay, you must plan carefully for three days how you intend to do this. On the fourth day begin the restorations. After starting, do not be distracted from your course of corrective action for the next three days. This is the time required to establish the new habit or way of thinking.

Relationships If the matter enquired about involves other people, then they have to be made aware of the corruption and misinformation. Then these people need to be motivated to find the strength and energy needed to change things. All types and levels of relationships are strained at this time. The problems confronting people have been caused by human ineptitude, or opinions, ideas and activities based on incorrect information. This state of affairs possibly came about because of incorrect attitudes imposed on people by their parents or guardians when they were young. This situation leaves people questioning, doubting, confronting, and re-evaluating all of their relationships. Once everything is out in the open, relationships can be formed on a new, open and solidly built foundation.

Romance and marrying is complicated; an old man with a young girl; a young man with an older woman; there is love but no union.

Travel is arduous. Travel only if it is necessary, or part of new initiatives being taken to overcome the decay, or to a place where the source of decay is located. Travelling for pleasure, or to avoid fixing the decay, is not a good idea.

Marketplace The marketplace is in a bad state but growth in business, career and academia will come about with new infrastructure and rebuilding. Get rid of anything or anyone that is outmoded, corrupt or not performing in a satisfactory manner. In business, rethinking management, organisation, systems, and products will revitalise the finances. Changing company or business policy will bring improvements to all.

Political parties should re-organise themselves and allow new elements to lead.

19 *Lin* 臨

Lin means approach, descend, attend, reach, visit, preside over, look kindly on; near to, during; while. **Lin** shows a kindly, benevolent statesman or official creating rank, order and classifications between groups and goods.

Image To arrive at the beginning ...

In the field *Lin's* image is of spring fast approaching; the time when farmers make ready for the growing season from spring to autumn. In ancient times, the affairs of the coming solar and lunar year were studied and the order of work prepared. Preparatory jobs such as tilling the field were begun.

Flow Yang energy – positive chi – is on the move, growing and pushing you along the path. Go with the flow; work with this energy while it is available. It's a loving, kind energy, which makes it the perfect time to approach something or someone; an opportunity that does not wait around forever.

Situations, ideas and projects begin to take form. Seeds become seedlings.

Look ahead and create a plan of action. Progress is joyous, hopeful and safe.

You will arrive at your destination.

Wealth Like the farmer, you must be ready to 'make hay while the sun shines'. The success of a quest for wealth of any kind seems certain and it is true that you will achieve the goal needed for acquiring wealth, but this is a short term proposition as conditions concerning the source of your wealth will change (that is, you might begin a new job and within a year your employer unexpectedly goes out of business). You must work with great energy and determination to make full use of these energy flows while they are here. At the autumn equinox, the energy that propels *Lin* forward begins its retreat into the earth again and a perfect wealth-creating opportunity disappears for another cycle. Be careful and use the wealth acquired in the time of *Lin* wisely; its source will dry up.

Relationships The harmonious chi created in the time of *Lin* enables people to communicate ideas and instructions clearly and to understand one another easily. This is a good time for two people to join forces to achieve a mutually held goal. This alliance will be made much easier if both parties can co-operate with each other and coordinate their activities.

Whether it is a business, personal or love relationship that you have enquired about, if two people want to join forces, they should do it now. Don't wait. Don't put it off, or else it won't happen. The cycle moves on, conditions change.

This is a good time for visiting and meeting friends. All social activities will go well. People meet each other for the first time or are still in the early stages of a relationship and getting to know each other. There is the first flush of antici-pation, of future possibilities.

There is news of travellers and people not seen for a long time. There is peace at home.

Travel Travel for any reason enriches you but long-distance travel should be completed by the autumn equinox.

Marketplace Create rank, order and classification between groups and goods.

Make lists, organise affairs, agendas and calendars.

Business is good for those involved in ice, ice rinks and ice-skating.

Music that is written, rehearsed or recorded, or in any way prepared for public consumption at this time, will bring prosperity.

Any short-term enterprise initiated now will show a good profit.

Working for the government or government aid is possible.

Any work that is in harmony with the season that you are in when you receive this Insight will be beneficial.

Feng shui Marshy ground, not good land to build on.

20 Guan

Guan means a view, an observatory, spectacle, a lookout, a Daoist temple; look at, see, view, inspect, display. **Guan**'s components are **Ren**: person; **Ch'ien**: opinion, see, view, perceive, meet with; **Ku**: ancient, primitive, old; **Chia**: beautiful, splendid, exquisite, superior; **Ku**: value, price. (A person sees an ancient beautiful thing of value or a person values an ancient, beautiful thing.)

Image Observation, contemplation. An overview.

In the field In ancient times, Yin Hi had an insight that a holy person was coming his way. He built a grass hut on the side of a pass through the western mountains as a lookout to observe all the people who travelled through the pass. Lao-tsu, the founder of Daoism, was departing China through this western pass, riding on an ox; Yin Hi recognized Lao-tsu as the holyman he had been waiting for and became his disciple.

Reputedly, it was to Yin Hi that Lao-tsu gave the teachings concerning dao– the book now called the *Dao de King*. It was from Yin Hi's grass hut meaning 'lookout' that Daoist temples derived their name.

Flow Look all around. Observe the stars and moon, the course of the seasons, the movement of creatures and people. Observe the balance of things. Observe your surroundings, the conduct of people around you and examine yourself. Observe the effect or influence you have created on those around you. Think carefully about what you have observed, note the changes that need to be made, and act upon them.

Curb any negative tendencies, and update or remove the outdated. Contemplate the effects of what has been produced. Then you will know the seeds of the future.

Suitable seeds must be sown at the opportune moment. Do not miss the right moment.

Wealth is ready and waiting (expectantly) for you to take it.

Opportunities should be acted on now while there is such harmony and support about for your endeavours. You are really very capable and prepared, even though you may not think so – those around you wait for your action. Take a moment of great concentration to focus all your energies before moving into action. Learn to meditate.

There is recovery from a long-term illness.

Relationships The right partner is close at hand. Have a good look around – you will find the person you are looking for. All types of current relationships and any relationships formed at this time will be supportive and clear-sighted. All misunderstandings will disappear.

It is the right time for fertilisation and a good month for insemination.

Travel Travellers are well-received wherever they go. Going on any type of pilgrimage will be beneficial.

Marketplace The marketplace requires a patient outlook and excellent foresight. In your business and career, it is time for review and analysis. Observe all facets of your enterprise, get an overview and update or remove accordingly. Plan the future path of the enterprise and then set the wheels rolling. Business begun in this way will prosper more slowly in the beginning, but because of its solid foundation, it will continue to prosper and grow for a very long time.

It is a good time to change jobs or careers for the better.

Prosperity will be found in the areas of literature, art and music. It is a good time for work, study or religious activity.

Feng shui If you have enquired about home or business premises to rent or buy, there is a two-storey building with good views and pleasant feng shui waiting for you to find it.

Miscellaneous The letter you are expecting arrives. You find what you are looking for.

21 Shi He 籌嗑

Shi He means 'biting through something that is covered or hidden'. The components are **Kou**: mouth; **Shi**: to bite, to eat; **shi:** to divine using yarrow stalks, **He**: drink, bite, chew, the sound of voices, and **He:** a covered vessel.

Image Law in the marketplace. Quality control. Fair trade. Consuming. Consumers. Consumerism.

In the field There is movement in the marketplace. The farmer has come to market to sell a top-quality crop and purchase some supplies. It is an important time for the farmer, who must make the profit from the crop and supplies purchased last until another crop is harvested and sold.

The market is abuzz with sounds, smells, products and people of every variety. At first the farmer has to work his way around the market and through the red tape. Traders try to dupe the farmer into selling the crop under the regulated market value or into buying sub-standard supplies at twice the market regulated price. But the farmer is clear-thinking, energetic and persistent so that all goes well in the end.

Flow *Shi He* talks about energetically biting through an obstacle that prevents a union of any kind. There are troubles at the beginning, when you can't understand why certain obstacles are appearing in your path. Then you have success when you discover the hidden and underhanded source of the obstacle, and energetically remove it.

Wealth *Shi He* energy brings clarity, energy and creativity. There is wealth available on all levels but it is not going to fall into your lap. There is lots of hard, energetic work and action needed. Lateral thinking will be beneficial. A person who has been starved of the nourishment they require is finally 'fed' and is momentarily content.

Relationships You should try to divine circumstances and events occurring around you that are hidden or not easily seen. There is a lot of tension in the air. The current energy is such that people are easily angered and quarrel. There are obstructions because a devious person will interfere and mislead. This sort of obstruction will not disappear by itself – you must take action! Use litigation if necessary. The time is favourable for the enforcement of justice. Lawsuits will be settled in your favour.

A third person comes between husband and wife.

Travel is successful but not smooth. A clear mind and lots of energy will be required. Take this book and the Insights on the journey, they may be needed. It is best to travel alone at this time.

Marketplace Any obstacles that impede a civilised, sociable, profitable, quality-controlled union of people must be overcome. All business, trade and commerce is active will profit if they abide by lawful marketplace practices.

Rules, regulations, conditions and penalites should be clearly displayed and enforced.

The food market, meat market, metal and gold all benefit. Open-air markets also benefit.

A legal career or involvement in legal matters is possible and successful at this time. There is plenty of work for ombudsmen and arbitrators.

Miscellaneous In contradiction to most other interpretations of *Yi Jing* Insights, I have always found that #21 *She He* refers to civil lawsuits and #6 *Sung* refers to criminal law.

22 Bi 賁

Bi means warrior; energetic, strenuous; bright, elegant, large, great; adorn. Its components are; **Bi**: (formal) beautifully adorned. **Bei**: shellfish, cowrie, money. **Chi**: ten; **Cao**: grass, plants, flowers; and **Mo**: alfalfa, clover, lucerne.

Image The star of happiness shines on you – the time is favourable.

Field The farmer has made a good profit from crop sales. Music is played joyfully as people relax, enjoy a glass of wine and watch the sunset. They observe the night sky and ponder the transformations of the seasons through the movement of the stars. Winter is approaching – it is time to prepare warm clothes, do any decorating or repair required in home or work environments, and organise the essential resources needed for winter.

Flow On one hand, *Bi* talks about the external world and taking care of small, current or immediate matters; taking care of essential 'bread and butter' matters that ensure your survival and well-being in the material world. On the other hand, *Bi* speaks of big issues and profound questions that need deep, deep thought and contemplation; deep transformations of the spirit; internal jewels or decorations that are perpetual and eternal.

You have arrived at a stage where there is relief from stress, tension and work. The mood is relaxed and you enjoy a well-deserved respite from activity, but this period should be regarded only as a short, very enjoyable, interlude. Keep up with current affairs and prepare for the next phase of action in your endeavours before these pleasant conditions change. Continued success comes through continuous effort and work.

At this stage your endeavours begin to change shape,

style and appearance. Don't get too carried away with the outward appearance of things at this time — content is definitely more important. Use decorum in small matters and keep large matters simple. It is important at this time to be self-sufficient and this is most easily achieved by keeping things simple. Try to avoid ostentation and don't give yourself 'airs and graces'.

Bi also says that in the early stages of an endeavour, conforming outwardly in dress and manner to the circumstances that surround you will advance your cause. Later on there will come a time when your personal philosophy and path can be shown safely.

Wealth There is wealth on all levels of your being. In the material world there is financial relief after a lean, tense time. Try not to overspend on non-essential items or fritter away resources; think about the bills and requirements which will come later on.

Meditation at this time is rewarding, illuminating and inspiring.

Relationships Avoid exhaustion from too much talk and razzle-dazzle.

Romance and marriage are lovely. Any type of partnership enquired about will work out well.

Travel will be delightful if travellers take care of all their current business and personal affairs before departing.

Marketplace With all these people around with money in their pockets, business will get better and better. Retail items positioned for 'impulse' buying (near checkouts and at the front of a store) will sell very well.

Packaging, labels or displays should be decorative and clearly indicate that a product is new or has been changed or updated in some way. The product itself should be simple, elegant and unpretentious.

Advertising, public relations, artists and creative people benefit. It is also a good time for astronomers. Musicians have plenty of work.

23 Bo 剝

Bo means to strip, skin, tear, peel off, extort, demand by force. Bo's components are **Jen**: edge, knife; **Po**: divine, foretell; **Xuan**: purple/black, profound, mysterious, incorporating concepts of occult and mysticism; **Shui**: water (symbolising the sub-conscious); and **Chu**: request, demand, ask, pray.

Image No support. Movement in any direction is unfortunate. It is unfavourable to undertake anything except spiritual activity.

In the field Nothing is growing.

Flow Unless you are asking about spiritual enlightenment in this life, or religious activities, the answer to your question is a big NO. Don't do it!

If possible, don't even get out of bed! This is a time when the smart thing to do is stay quiet and avoid action. When the time of splitting apart has passed (and you will easily recognise it when it has), you will again achieve influence and effectiveness; supported by public opinion.

If *Bo* represents a situation you are already in, remember that at certain times in life this *Bo* process must occur so that one can grow. In the time of *Bo* there is great inner learning. Virtue DOES generate its own rewards. When these bad times pass, grief becomes joy. Keep the faith. *Bo* will present you with an opportunity to do something to The Good; something you have always intended to do.

Wealth Apart from spiritual wealth, there isn't any. However, in your darkest monetary moment, women or a woman will give assistance and you will escape the troubles.

Bo brings about the understanding and removal of illusions that you have been harbouring for a long time. In all matters, examine the reality of structure and frame. Examine the true skeleton.

If you did ask about enlightenment and spiritual matters; you are in the right place at the right time. In the Heavenly scheme of things, *Bo* is where Gotama, the soon to be Buddha, decided to sit, beneath the Buddhi tree, until he became enlightened or died trying. He succeeded and arose as Buddha, whereupon he sang a song about overcoming sorrows and delusions.

Relationships In romance, marriage and partnerships in general, things are not what they seem to be; people are not being truthful. Jealous, devious people abound; they use sneaky, nefarious methods to achieve their goals. Opportunities are therefore not what they seem. However, you still have some true friends who will support and help you through this crisis. Women come to your aid. Generosity to those less fortunate than yourself is not a mistake.

Travel If your life looks OK at this time, and you are thinking of travelling for business or pleasure, don't do it, as this is where the splitting apart will occur; nothing will be as anticipated. Even if cancelling this trip costs you money, delays and hassles, don't go. If you do go on this trip, hang onto your hat, keep the faith and be sure to take this book and the Insights with you – they will be needed.

If you are already experiencing the conditions described in *Bo*, you might move to another place, area or country to escape these difficulties. This move will be greatly to your benefit and you will prosper there.

Marketplace Definitely not the time to expand business or advance your career. Work and business prospects do not look good. Conditions will improve in a couple of months.

Pay attention to the maintenance of your transport.

Security services prosper.

Feng shui The prognosis for property is not good – check the roof. It is not a sturdy structure, and may be in danger of collapsing. The general framework of the building needs serious attention.

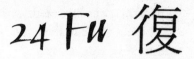

24 Fu 復

Fu means return, repeat, restore, turn around, recover, resume, a second time, again. Its components are the **60th radical**: person of worth; **Chi**: step, walk; **Shi**: follow; and **Jih**: the sun.

Image At the starting point again.

In the field Picture the winter solstice in China when the weather is bitterly cold and snowy. In ancient times, the Chinese rulers closed the entrances to their states and provinces. Doors were shuttered and gates were closed. People used to stay indoors and not much business was done. There were celebrations marking the winter solstice as nature's turning point, heralding the return of light and energy. *Daoists* performed the Rite of Cosmic Renewal and Peace to wipe away evil. In the high mountains, the peasants ceremoniously danced, sang, and scattered seeds inside their temple to propitiate the returning life force. Farmers rested, gathering energy for the fast-approaching spring, planning the coming year's crop, organising their equipment and resources, and doing internal maintenance. Deep within the earth the first germs of new life were awakening.

Flow Yang creative energy (chi) stirs dormant life. Thoughts and ideas that have lain dormant within begin to vibrate. The energy is in the lowest chakra. This is the beginning of new growth and light – it must be nurtured, protected and allowed to grow (just like a baby in the womb).

Seeds of new beginnings. The seed subsumes the tree. *Fu* subsumes all that will grow in the coming cycle. It is a very important time. Seeds ideas, projects – whatever is planned for your 'field'; all must be nurtured. The first step or steps will be the most important. Now is the time to establish what it is you want to achieve in the coming cycle and how you intend to do it. Stimulate energy and 'seed' growth with a generally quiet life. Stick to routine and stay close to home.

Expect to hear about the matter or person enquired about within seven days.

Wealth The darkest day has passed – you have reached the turning point. A shimmer of new light sparks into life. This is the beginning of a new cycle. Now is the time for planning wealth, selecting a direction, focusing on it and honing the tools or skills needed to achieve it. Indoor activities, as well as mental, intellectual, creative, and spiritual activities, are highly successful and deeply rewarding. The creative force is generating and germinating in all spheres of your being. Success comes after preparation and nurturing. A debt owed to you will be repaid. The money or resources needed to see you through will arrive or appear. Financial matters slowly take a turn for the better. Illness begins to disappear.

Relationships Generally, people are tired. Tiredness leads to muddled thinking. So don't change an existing plan, appointment or written material that was already organised before you drew this Insight.

A good time for visiting friends locally. People of clarity, vision, sound judgement and fortitude are around you. There will be a feast with family or friends. This is a stimulating event but don't overdo it as over-the-top activity will sap your incoming energy. Spend as much time as possible alone. You should listen to your inner self and be good to yourself. See if a very private 'party' can be organised where you are the only guest. Light a new candle to symbolise the spark of creative energy stirring within you.

Be generous and sharing with your resources now and you will have willing helpers when you need them. Be cool; right now is not a good time to let on how much you understand about a situation occurring in your environment; keep it to yourself. When difficulties, confusion or misunderstandings arise, take the time to trace the problem back to its source; return to the starting point; get to the root of the matter.

It is easy to fall pregnant at this time.

Travel A good time for local travel, short outings and journeys; not good for overnight or long-distance travel.

Marketplace Business is quiet now but it will soon be much busier. Use this time for internal maintenance and review. Consider new ideas, stock and resources, and prepare a business plan and strategy for the coming year or cycle.

It is a good time of good fortune for cultural activities, organisers, promoters, and entrepreneurs.

Travelling salespeople, officials and magistrates should take a break and stay at home.

Inventors and innovative thinkers are in the right place at the right time.

Literary and artistic efforts and pursuits succeed.

Hardware stores do great trade.

Archery clubs thrive and archery accessories sell very well.

It is not a good time for digging or excavating.

Products or items that are elaborately made, or are considered to be luxury goods, should be avoided at this time.

Study and academia come easily. Students pass exams.

Miscellaneous One cold, windy, rainy night I had arrangements to go to a late concert in the city, but I wanted to stay snuggled up at home doing some writing. I was home alone and already being nice to myself with a long, hot bubble bath. I consulted the Insights and received *Fu* which described the weather and my feelings perfectly, but said don't change existing plans. So off I went to the concert. I had a great time and caught up with friends I hadn't seen for ages. We ended up having an enormous feast in a Chinese restaurant, and some of the group decided to go dancing afterwards. I remembered what *Fu* said about not pushing things too far and opted to go home, but the whole thing left me invigorated and motivated, with several new ideas running through my brain. Within a year, these ideas had turned into tangible, profitable ventures.

25 Wu Wang 无妄

Wu means no, nothing, nil, not having, there is not, without, not.
Wang means erroneous, false, wrong, foolish, absurd; error, blame; not wrong.

Image Whilst innocently attending to your own affairs in a correct and timely fashion, something unexpected or unintentional occurs; something happens that is not correct but at the same time not wrong, and brings supreme success.

In the field Life energy begins to move again; everything starts to sprout and grow. The farmer plants out the field, doing all that needs to be done for an abundant crop without calculating the result of the harvest. There could be floods, droughts, fires or pestilence to wipe out crop at any stage before harvest comes.

Flow A person's mind is natural and true with no ulterior motives or secret agendas. Such a person does the right thing with instinctive sureness, without thought of reward or personal gain – this brings supreme success.

With *Wu Wang*, 'not wrong', whatever has been enquired of will come about in an unexpected manner. Or something unexpected, something not enquired about, will happen very soon and has over-ridden that matter that you have enquired about. Don't be alarmed or put out by the unexpected, try take it with good grace. It is a cliché but undoubtedly the universe is unfolding as it should – keep faith.

Wealth Inner strength, common sense, innate intelligence and communication skills abound! There will be profit, learning and good fortune, on all levels of being.

Confidently follow the original impulses of the heart, or that initial gut feeling, assured of good fortune and achievement of your aims. Everything should occur naturally without design; don't try to calculate the results. If difficulties are encountered, be adaptable rather than struggling against the current. Make sure that all the things that you are personally responsible for are in shipshape order, and tidy or clean your home or immediate environment as soon as possible if it needs doing.

Illness cures itself and needs no medicine.

Relationships Unexpected troubles may come to your door. Be calm – these are not troubles of your own making or doing and will disappear as suddenly as they arrived. These troubles are not part of your karma; they belong to somebody else's karma; somebody you have been caught up with. You are just a bit player in the cosmic play.

Love and marriage are not happy. Current partnerships are difficult. Any type of new partnership under consideration at this time will not prosper or grow.

Travel Journeys bring profit in an unexpected manner. Check all travel details carefully. There are thieves about. Keep important possessions close to you, in your hand luggage or on your person. Travel insurance is a good idea and clearly label all baggage.

Marketplace Gain fame and reputation through creative business efforts.

Entering into new agreements at this time will not improve profits. Keep all work up-to-date – make your business environment sparkle and shine. Unexpected business, or business that comes about through unusual circumstances, is on the way.

Watch out for shoplifters, pickpockets and thieves.

Miscellaneous The events that occur in the time of *Wu Wang* help to prepare you or the person enquired about, for a large and important endeavour in the future.

26 Da Chu 大畜

Together the characters **Da Chu** mean great nourishment or a great offering. Individually, **Da** means great, huge, gigantic, chief, important; **Chu** means raise, nourish, domesticate, keep in store, domestic animals, livestock. **Chu**'s components are **Tian**: field; and **Xuan**: purple, profound, mysterious.

Image Hugely profound mysteries appear in the field. The flow of chi is right for a cosmic connection. Nourishing the invisible in order to nourish the visible.

In the field In ancient times, the Emperor, the Son of Heaven, ascended to his Ancestral Cave on the Mountain. Animals were slaughtered and offered in a great ceremony to nourish his Ancestors whilst sages and saddhus, seeing the transitoriness of all things, ascended to caves on the Mountain to nourish their inner selves. Scholars in retreat nourished their intellect.

Flow Now is the time to nourish your inner and outer self to accumulate the strength, knowledge and energy needed for some big undertakings later on. If there are unfinished tasks or 'business', now is the time to complete them. There is a lot of work to be done, with dilemmas and obstacles along the way, but even difficult and/or dangerous enterprises will succeed.

Da Chu says to look for solutions, strategies and new ideas by remembering deeds and events in your past. Look at the knowledge you have accumulated in your life; remember how the successes were achieved and where the failures and the pitfalls were. *Da Chu* also suggests considering words of wisdom from ancient sources as another source of solutions or ideas. This could be anything from religious texts, historical works, myths or legends through to something that your grandmother or other elderly person told/tells you.

Wealth There is news of good luck.

For the success of your enquiry, you need to be objectively

involved with other people. Activities that take you outside of your home environment are in harmony with the time and will succeed. Employment in a public, commercial or corporate setting is part of the knowledge-gathering activities needed now for great deeds later. This is not the time to be holed up by yourself or in a totally domestic environment.

Spiritually, you can make great advances at this time. Yogic or Daoist breathing exercises refine the inner nature, purifying the mind and clarifying the senses.

Sickness eases.

Relationships This is a time to be in the public eye; don't eat at home, be out and about. Friendliness will win people over.

Attending or holding a large dinner for many people in a public place (restaurant) benefits you.

Family members understand one another.

Quarrels are pacified.

Marriage is good. Any type of relationship will go well.

Travel Journeys bring understanding and good fortune but be careful on the roads; do not drive aggressively. Attend to your car; there may be trouble with the axle and/or wheels. If you are buying a car, make sure it is a sturdy one.

Marketplace All types of enterprises can attract a lot of customers and make great gains. But first you need to get out there in the marketplace and sell yourself and your product. Go to every business function available; talk to people; network. Hold an information evening or workshop on your product, do some promotions. Advertise! At first your enterprise may experience frustrating constraints and delays that hamper growth. These conditions will change without you needing to apply any force. Soon business will prosper, and will be further enhanced by creative efforts. But be cautious; ensure all the necessary steps are taken to protect your business: patents, contracts naming rights, maintenance, investment.

A Chinese astrology chart is of benefit.

The gold and metal market benefits and prospers.

27 Yi 臣頁

Yi means the chin, the cheek, nourish, rear, take care of one's health. One of its components is **Yeh**: page, sheet, folio; a component of **Yeh** is **Bei**: wealth, a Buddhist book.

Image Nourishment. Care of what goes in and out of the mouth. Careful of words.

In the field There are tigers on the mountain and oxen in the field. The farmer is at work ploughing; creating nourishment for physical survival. But it's still early spring and there is a lot of work to be done before harvest. Nourishment and good fortune comes with effort.

Flow Yi talks about nourishment for mind, body and soul and the acquisition of it.

Try to be temperate in your eating and drinking. Watch what you and others eat, how it is prepared, who prepared it and the way in which it is eaten. All types of food affect the quality of your thoughts; and the quality of your thoughts creates the words that you speak.

Yi talks about a person who understands the correct nourishment needed and tries to find it. This person receives the nourishment from a holy person or teacher. Afterwards this person is able to nourish lots of other ordinary people by providing them with the holy person's teachings.

Finally *Yi* talks about a person who achieves sagehood or an advanced understanding of the nourishment needed and how to get it. People will look up to this person and follow him or her. This person has to always be aware of the responsibility placed upon him or her.

Wealth Be assured you have the ability, and the blessings of Heaven, to live independently. Don't give up your self-reliance or forget your personal 'magic'. You are quite capable of providing your own 'nourishment', you do not need others to provide it. Your search for riches will succeed, and wealth on all levels comes as a result of hard work. You have the ability to correctly pinpoint the source of problems.

The constant pursuit of sense – gratification desires is debilitating, not nourishing.

Illness disappears.

Relationships To know what another person considers important, observe and listen to that person. What do they talk about consistently and repeatedly? Note their actions over a period of time. For whom or what do they give care and attention? What side of their nature do they cultivate? Is this person someone you should be involved with?

Travel Travelling by plane or water is not recommended at this time. Journeys by land are good. A meeting with sage-like, wise people on a riverbank brings great good fortune and prosperity.

Marketplace Success in your career with the help of another – there will be no more difficulties.

Commerce is good. Creative efforts will be highly successful.

For students – small jobs now, but later a high position and good fortune.

Miscellaneous In 1983 just before leaving to go on a spiritual sojourn through Asia, a friend consulted the *I Ching* about me and the outcome of my travels. *Yi* was the answer. At the time it made both of us laugh because I was actually eating my dinner whilst he was doing the *I Ching*. But now as I read the Ancient Insights version of *Yi*, I can see there was a lot more to it. I did meet sage-like people on a riverbank (in Varanasi, India). I did receive nourishment from a holy person and I have been able to nourish lots of other people by providing them with the holy person's teachings, that is, this book. But I think I still have a way to go before I get to the sagehood part – perhaps another life.

28 Da Gua 大過

Together, the characters **Da Gua** mean great excess. Individually, **Da** means great, huge, gigantic, chief, important. **Gua** means error, fault, mistake; pass, cross, go by, pass through; too, excessively; over, above, beyond; go beyond (a certain point of time); spend time, pass time; undergo a process.

Image An unusual situation, greatly beyond the ordinary. Extraordinary times.

In the field The farmer's load is too heavy for its supports. The farmer must find some ways to move some of the load as quickly as possible before the load breaks.

Flow Something must be moved or it will break. Success comes if you have a purpose or goal. Maybe it is time for a new purpose or goal. Unusual efforts or ideas will make progress possible. *Da Gua* counsels that exceptional caution and care are needed in laying proper foundations at the beginning of an enterprise. Your ambitions may be greater than your current abilities, so do things little by little.

Sometimes something must be done which might be beyond your normal strength and capacity. However, now is the right time to attempt this feat; Heaven will lend assistance.

Wealth Relief from the load created by lack of wealth comes from an innovative idea or unusual activity. It leads to a wealth of knowledge, and a prosperous, lasting path. Somebody helps when needs are communicated.

Like everything else in the time of *Da Gua*, something has to be moved. This could be something as simple as moving money from one account to another account where a debit is due.

In health matters, doing or eating too much of one thing should be avoided.

Relationships Marriage affairs are not good; there is an older man and a young woman or an older woman with a younger man. Although two people love each other dearly, it is hard for them to find happiness. A man is involved with two women, an older woman (probably his wife) and a much younger woman.

It is time for a serious talk with all types of partners. Avoid arrogance, aggression and one-sidedness.

Join with people of lesser standing for success.

Travel It is a good time to move something, somebody or maybe yourself, to another place. Relief and success will be found there.

Marketplace There is too much of something in one place, which usually means that there is not enough of something in another place. Perhaps business or business advertising should be moved to another place where there isn't enough of a product or service. Business can be moved but it should not be expanded. A new action or enterprise brings success when care is taken in establishing its foundations.

Move things, change things, don't leave too much of anything in one place. Update; get rid of outdated or outmoded methods and non-renewable systems.

Products with an average price range do best.

Disputes may occur with employees overloaded with work. It is in the employer's best interests to rearrange the workload so it is balanced more evenly amongst all the staff.

Check all connections and don't leave loose ends.

Take care in or near bodies of water.

Feng shui If asking about house or land, don't buy it or move there. There is trouble with supports and foundations. A real estate speculator ignored this advice when he received *Da Gua* and purchased the property anyway. It turned out that the property was built on landfill that had not been packed properly. An air bubble popped and the building tilted into the hole. I drew *Da Gua* before going to a Feng Shui consultation. When I walked through the front door of the property I fell through the rotting floorboards!

29 Kan 坎

Kan means a bank or a ridge; pit, hole. Kan's components are Tu: earth, ground, land; region, territory, native, local, particular to the place; and Chien: yawning, deficient, wanting, lacking; owe.

Image If your heart is sincere and true, whatever you do (to escape danger) will succeed.

In the field Someone is caught in a pit or a ravine with fast-flowing water rushing through it. There are mountains/rocks on one side and dense, tiger-riddled jungle on the other side. Danger.

Flow Get out of a (metaphysical or metaphorical) pit or difficult situation by acting like water. Water's natural direction is downwards; when it encounters a pit, it fills it and moves on its way. Water infiltrates rather than dominates; it is unobtrusively persistent. Most importantly, water keeps moving; going forward, not tarrying in danger.

If your (spiritual) heart is good and true, whatever you do will be successful. These are most important words in *Kan*. Do you have a sincere heart in the matter you have enquired about? Consider this carefully. Are your motives true? Are you being true to yourself? Maintain confidence and keep a sharp hold on the mind. An objective, not subjective, attitude is what is needed. Look objectively at the situation. Carry out all that needs to be done. Thoroughness in everything will bring good fortune.

Wealth You get the essential wealth you need on any level of being. Strive for small things only; don't be too ambitious at this time; be content to be in a safe space.

Simple, sincere kindnesses to your neighbours bring benefits for everybody.

At this time your communication skills are excellent. You have the ability to keep things flowing by utilising the talents and resources of others. Make use of social contacts and networking.

You lose at gambling.

Relationships There are many hazards in your environment; there is trickery and deceit around. Be careful and patient.

All types of new unions, partnerships and relationships should be put on hold for the time being.

You cannot find the person you are looking for at this time.

Teenagers and young men metaphysically, and sometimes literally, howl at the moon. Their hormones are raging and they think they are invincible.

Travel It is not a good time for travel by water.

Take great care when crossing roads or driving. Young male drivers are hazardous at this time.

Marketplace The energy provided by *Kan* gives the enquirer the ability to note things that will become important, and accurately assess the potential of future ideas or projects. But now is not the time to do anything about them. In business and investment, there are many pits and hazards to be avoided. It is not the time for big deals, projects or enterprises; be happy to cover your costs and survive. Don't begin new business or enterprises. Guard against robbery, burglary, flood or water damage.

It is not a good time for swimming, water sports, rock climbing or absailing.

An excellent time for teaching, learning, studying, researching, and for religious studies and writings — there is a cauldron of knowledge waiting.

Avoid narrow or deep or dark places.

Feng shui A place where an accident is just waiting to happen. If this is a place where you live or work, put up a small bagua mirror as an immediate 'band-aid' solution and consult a feng shui practitioner.

30 *Li* 離

Li means leave, separate; a yellow bird of brilliant plumage; from (in giving distance); without, independent of. **Li's** components are the **radicals** for cocoon and cover; **Feng**: wind; **Chui**: short-tailed birds; and **Li**: bright, elegant, a ghost.

Image To separate and to cling to. Eyes. Yellow light is seen – supreme good fortune.

In the field Everything in the universe depends upon something else for its survival. This is a natural law of the universe. The abundant and perfect crop that is ready for harvesting in the field grew successfully with the right amount of sunlight, rain and generally favourable weather conditions. The farmer understands this, honouring the sun as the source of the crop's survival and success.

Flow There is glory and brightness; nature in all its radiance. *Li* represents fire and light, and the sun as the one source of both. At the beginning of something, be cautious, watch your step and where you put your foot. Try to find the middle way of action between extremes. *Li* is a very emotional and volatile Insight. People are suddenly happy, then sad, then excited, then dejected and crying, before discovering things are going to be alright anyway. Catastrophies are not going to happen.

Wealth Your mind is bright and clear, your energy levels are high and your actions are intelligent. Your brightness can illuminate the four corners of the world and you have great successes. Wealth shines brightly in all realms of your being. Now is the time to harvest while the 'crops' are at their peak of growth. Like the farmer at this time, it is important that you acknowledge the source of your dependence and light.

Li's energy brings clarity and spiritual perception. Dharma, the right action, is the order of the day. You can easily control the physical senses at this time if you want to. Being able to distinguish between things so clearly right now means it's an excellent time for creative, intellectual pursuits. Illness disappears. Herbal cures are beneficial.

Relationships All types of relationships and partnerships formed at this time are clear-sighted and succeed. In romantic matters, go for it! Make that commitment to each other now – don't hesitate.

You make good progress in specialised matters of interest to you and find a way for others, also interested in the same specialised areas, to continue and extend your work or research.

People are happy to know the enquirer or the person enquired about.

Travel is illuminating and successful. Also see the travel section of #56 *Lu* the traveller.

Marketplace The marketplace radiates with wonderful products and prosperity. Business is profitable. Working impartially, without favouritism for a particular person, group or product, brings good fortune.

All facets of the lighting industry experience good fortune; as does the solar and electric power industry. Anything concerning eyes and vision, cameras and visual-audio equipment brings prosperity. Farmers will prosper. Artisans will make a profit.

Any activity or person connected with horses benefits.

If employed, you will soon be given an important position. Public servants and officials will be promoted. Those looking for work get the job they want.

Exams will be passed with recognition.

Check scales, weights and measures for accuracy.

Take care with fire.

Feng shui Check the electrics at the property thoroughly. Consider fire safety. If possible, the garden should be designed to reduce hazard from bush fire.

Miscellaneous Something that arouses and excites you during the first 15 days of the 5th moon month is an illusionary, transitory thing that is soon forgotten.

31 Xian / Gan 咸

Xian means all, whole, altogether. **Xian**'s components are **Kou** meaning mouth, opening; the **radical** for cliff; and **Ge** meaning lance. Ancient sages say the title should be **Gan** not **Xian**. **Gan** means feel, sense, affect, influence. **Gan** is drawn as **Xian** but with **Sin**, meaning heart, added.

Image Preparing for something you hope and wish will happen as if it is definitely going to happen. Mind power and positive thinking.

In the field There is stimulating growth and development. The farmer's youngest daughter and the youngest son of a neighbouring farmer are deeply attracted to each other and wish to marry. The fathers aren't decided on the matter; they have yet to reach an agreement about the dowry and the like. Formal contracts have not yet been exchanged, but the girl is accumulating items in a glory box to use in her household after she marries and the boy prepares a household for her. They are both practising positive thinking.

Flow *Xian/Gan* suggests that goals can be achieved by focusing on them mentally and visualising their achievement, whilst physically preparing for the time when what you are trying to attract arrives. People and 'things' will be subtly drawn to you. *Gan* counsels that an idea or new project being considered needs a lot more thought before it is put into action. Prepare mentally to be open and receptive to new ideas and advice. Then there will be stimulating development and potential in the matter enquired about.

In all areas and spheres of your life, small things are favoured. Check all details down to the smallest item for success. Events alluded to in *Gan/Xian* often happen very soon after the enquirer has drawn the Insight.

Wealth The real influence is taking place deep within your subconscious. Listen to this inner influence. Some tension and anxiety are the outward signs of this. For success, stay where you are now positioned. The area and scope of your influence increases. Try to be a self-sufficient individual and not run after those whom you wish to impress, nor pursue every desire that comes to the fore. Impulsive action at this time is not recommended. Instead, try to achieve a 'joyful stillness'.

Taking care of the physical body will benefit you. Practising yoga, tai chi or a similar slow exercise will be helpful. Meditation is also beneficial.

The contract or the cheque really is in the mail.

Relationships People are only temporarily influenced by talk; pretty soon they want to see action. They want to see what you keep saying you are going to do actually being done. Do the deed or stop talking about it. If thoughts and actions are not focused, only those friends who already know and understand you will be influenced. A 'know-it-all' type of person will find himself without help.

In social relationships, like will attract like and heartfelt attractions will occur. Consider the difference between seduction and courtship. An engagement to marry is announced. A young man and woman suit each other well and should marry.

Those absent send news.

Travel Dreaming about and preparing for future travel is more likely at this time than actually going travelling.

Marketplace Lines of communication are used. Taking preparatory action, such as drawing up contracts, agreements and job descriptions before forming unions and partnerships of all kinds, brings good fortune. Make sure everybody understands what is required of them. You should prepare now for the events that will follow the union or partnership.

If business or endeavours have been slow, don't be gloomy; act as if lots and lots of customers are expected. Make the business environment shipshape and shiny. Get a new invoice book ready for all the invoices that will be written. Organise extra staff on standby to deal with a rush of customers. Set all the tables in a restaurant even if there are no bookings. Tell the universe you are ready, prepared and happy to receive customers – they will come.

Feng shui Use some feng shui strategies; photos or items that symbolise what you are trying to attract, and put some small written affirmations about the place. Place your business card, business registration certificate or something bearing your name or logo on a wall facing north in the southern hemisphere or south in the northern hemisphere.

Miscellaneous My neighbour Martin was a very funny and good-hearted soul but he didn't take much interest in his personal grooming and hygiene, his flat was a pigsty, he was always in and out of lowly paid employment, and for the two years I had known him he was always talking about doing some educational courses to improve his prospects but that hadn't happened. He asked the Insights about finding a girl-friend and the answer was *Gan*. He straight away enquired about job prospects this time and again the answer was *Gan*. He said he didn't understand so I gave him some motherly advice – if he wanted to attract a girl he should take some trouble with his appearance and if he wanted a girl to come back to his flat he should clean it. If he wanted a good job, he had to do the further studies he was always talking about. He went away, insight in hand, slightly offended by my comments. But an hour later he came back and borrowed my vacuum cleaner and hair clippers. When he returned them – wow – was he looking sharp! About a week later we began to see him about the place with an attractive woman on his arm who eventually moved in with him. He began part-time further education courses and after his excellent first term results he applied for a job with the government and got it on the strength of his results and continuing studies.

32 Heng 恒

Heng means permanent, lasting, perseverance, usual, common, constant, perpetual, regular, fixed, continuously. **Heng's** component characters are **Miao**, meaning small; and **Keng** meaning universal; an extreme limit, the first or last quarter of the moon; fill or extend.

Image To make something permanent or long-lasting.

In the field In ancient times the Emperor, the Son of Heaven, lived in a palace with 800 buildings containing 9,000 rooms. He moved from room to room according to the time of day, season of the year, and the position of certain stars in the sky. He imitated the movements ordained by the Celestial Emperor of Heaven.

Flow The stars move through the heavens in fixed and re-occurring patterns. *Heng* suggests good fortune is found by following the stars' example; moving forward and progressing in the direction that you are already going in, but with a particular goal in mind, and doing this in an organised, fixed, routine manner similar to the orbiting planets.

To create a routine you must first establish what goal you are trying to achieve from this routine and what that routine is going to be. Then you must start following that routine. After this comes the tricky part when things pop up unexpectedly. Don't be distracted – stay focused.

Nobody will have faith in a person who keeps chopping and changing all the time. *Heng* says endure and remain constant. Restlessness will get you nowhere at this time and can actually endanger your endeavours.

Heng observes that it is unfortunate to continuously do something that has no enduring purpose or to keep looking for something in a place where it cannot be found. Utilise intuition and the *yin*, receptive, side of your being to discover an enduring goal, and seek the thing looked for in the north-western suburbs, area or direction in the southern hemisphere and to the south-west in the northern hemisphere. Be composed; coherent actions will bring success.

Wealth You attract and acquire wealth on all levels of your being with no trouble at all. Perform your role with ease – everything flows and long-lasting harmony and equilibrium is possible. Stability and regularity show the way at this time. Stay on course and stand firm. Do not change your current formula, tactics or line of activity.

Relationships Creating something that is permanent or lasting takes time and is never achieved overnight. People who seek permanence too quickly or without the proper foundations and preparations will end up in a mess. Marriage is enduring, loving, strong and prosperous. *Heng* is an excellent Insight to receive if you have enquired about marrying, a new romance or any type of union or partnership. It will be a solid relationship, prosperous, long-lasting and harmonious for the most part; quarrels will be easily settled.

Travel Journeys are favourable if they have a purpose and set direction but be adaptable regarding transport modes, timetables and routes.

Marketplace There is an opportunity here to make your business or endeavour flourish and grow for a long time. This is not the time to change the nature or direction of your business or endeavour but it is the time to set standards and targets. New enterprises and partnerships need firmly defined goals and outcomes established at the beginning. All businesses and endeavours need to be adaptable and flexible in the systems, tactics and methods used along the way to the achievement of these goals.

Advertise – some potential customers don't know where you are located.

Your career brings profits. Those employed can successfully change jobs for the better if they stay in their current line of work.

33 Dun 恒

Dun means hide, conceal oneself, go into obscurity, escape. **Dun**'s components are **Chen**: halt; **Yue**: moon; and **Shi**: pig (drawn as a pig's tail).

Image Retreat. Go into obscurity. Escape.

In the field In solar time, *Dun* refers to the end of summer. In ancient times, during this period, astronomers and sages retreated to high mountains to observe the revolution of the 'tail' of the Big Dipper star constellation around Tzu Wei, the pole star. Here begins the downward part of the Big Dipper's clockwise movement around the heavens, heralding the approach of autumn and winter.

Flow Withdrawal is the correct way to behave at this time in order not to exhaust your forces. This is a natural condition of time. Try to stay out of the public eye and the limelight. The *yin* force of winter is advancing. The creative force of summer is not seen; it goes into obscurity where it can consolidate its work and renew energy. So should you or the matter enquired about.

Sometimes you find yourself caught up in a situation that seems contrary to your essential nature and the course you wish to take. Many obscuring issues and events cloud and hamper the path. You should hold inwardly onto your ideals and beliefs as hard as you can; don't let go! *Dun* suggests that within the enquirer hides (divine) 'magic' and great power but it is important to disguise these qualities at this time.

Wealth No great profits at this time. Don't worry unduly; Heaven sees your inner worth and will aid and protect you.

A vegetarian diet is beneficial for you.

A Chinese astrology chart brings knowledge and insight.

You may encounter a great teacher or sage.

Acts of generosity or charity that you perform at this time

should be kept to yourself and not boasted or talked about, nor used as a tax deduction.

Relationships Sages, scholars, painters, writers, and the person enquired about should retreat to the mountains or other high, hard to reach places, both external and internal.

Displays of anger, even righteous anger, will not benefit you. Retreat from small-minded people and irritating situations mentally if you cannot retreat physically. This is not the time to contest an opponent directly. Your words may get you into trouble. Compromise or withdraw. Consider the Chinese virtue of saving face.

You may acquire an anticipated and unneeded employee. This slows your retreat down but there is not much that can be done about the situation for the time being.

A son is born.

Marriage is not likely at this time.

Nothing comes of a cooperative venture or partnership.

Peace talks, conferences, conventions and retreats are beneficial at this time.

Travel A trip to the mountains will be beneficial. Travel as a means of escaping a difficult situation is a good idea.

Marketplace New enterprises and projects do not benefit. Old enterprises and projects bring increase. Classical, historical and ancient enterprises benefit. For example, an antique furniture shop would do better than a modern furniture shop.

It is a good time for astronomers.

Theatres, restaurants, hotels, and the entertainment industry do good business; also conference and retreat venues. Facilitators also benefit.

Not a good time to undertake building projects.

Writers, artists and scholars will benefit if they can manage to stay out of the limelight and get some work done.

Your career moves slowly.

34 Da Zhuang 大壯

Da means great, big, huge, gigantic, chief, important; enlarge, grow large; highly, extremely, greatly. **Zhuang** means strong, robust, healthy, hardy, full-grown, fertile, thick, fat, muscular; in spirit; encourage, strengthen, embolden; invigorate. **Zhuang**'s components are **Ban** meaning plank; and **Shih** meaning an officer, a soldier, a gentleman, a scholar.

Image Great strength. You've got the power!

In the field The field needs its water levels steadily maintained, so an irrigation system is set in place. *Da Zhuang* depicts something that has been established in the field, that is already robustly healthy and fertile, being encouraged to become gigantically huge and important; being encouraged to become the chief.

Flow Creative energy pushes growth into abundance so fast that one can almost hear the crop that is growing so strongly in your 'field'. Activity follows a quiet period – good fortune. There are no entanglements – obstructions give way. The time is favourable for new actions and efforts.

It is a time of tangibles, 'see-ables'. Ideas and projects that you have been nourishing and nurturing have grown and progressed sufficiently to be transplanted into your 'big' field of endeavour. In the beginning, pay attention to the correct use of energy and power; channel things now so that they do not overwhelm you later. Your field of endeavour needs an 'irrigation system' organised to keep the energy levels, finances, production, and so on flowing smoothly. Your field of endeavour must be kept free of 'weeds'. Don't take short-cuts trying to make your endeavours grow faster. Persevere quietly to remove all obstacles to the abundant growth of your crop so that your 'seedlings' have the opportunity to become giganticly huge and important. But no boasting.

Wealth There is wealth and power in all realms of your being. Great strength and intelligence will work together to overcome great barriers. Your inner worth and achievements to date create a great and powerful force that ensures prosperous progress towards goals and abundant growth in your field. Whatever you do will be successful, but will also have ensuing consequences and karma. So make sure the actions you take at this time are to the good.

Illness is cured or goes into remission. Vitality levels are high.

Relationships With so much inner power at this time you must be careful not to intentionally, or unintentionally, take unfair advantage of others.

All partnerships respond to your wishes and quarrels are avoided.

Do not rush into marriage at this time.

If already married, kindness and patience bring harmony.

Travel All journeys are favourable, easy and fast.

Marketplace Business and all enterprises will succeed.

Large undertakings away from your regular field of endeavour will not benefit at this time.

The unemployed find work.

Students succeed in exams.

Ensure security systems are working.

Architects will benefit at this time.

Carpenters prosper after finding the right type of wood for their projects.

Things are looking good for farmers.

Musicians, singers and the music industry in general benefit at this time. Concerts go well.

Feng shui Check the roof and ceiling. Also check gutterings, drains and water channels. Ensure the security of your property.

35 Jin 晉

Jin means enter, advance, promote, increase, proceed. **Jin**'s components are **Jih**, meaning sun; and the **radical** for movement (like a flight of birds). The ancient character for **Jin** showed two birds flying toward the sun.

Image The sun rises over the earth. There is movement towards the light.

In the field A feudal prince swears loyalty to the king and is rewarded with horses and three audiences with his ruler in a single day. In ancient times during the summer, horses, which were a rare and precious commodity, were rounded up, broken in and then allocated to lords and officials, or traded.

Flow Time of beginnings with promise and hope for the future. Everything begins to fall into place now. The time is favourable for action; great results will be achieved.

Jin comments on the various stages of progressing. At first there could be obstructions, making progress, hard work. Maintain a calm, positive persona, keep an open mind, try lateral thinking, and try, try again. You will succeed and progress onwards. Feelings of loneliness or aloneness may arise along the way but there is no time available to play or socialise, no time to do other than all the tasks necessary at the beginning of progress. You know what needs to be done, so do it.

An opportunity may arise that your good and honest nature will not allow you to exploit. This may leave you with wistful thoughts of what might have been; let it go, let it pass, it is of no consequence. Your good and honest actions bring far greater success and influence in the future.

Stop every now and then to check your progress to date and fix glitches that may have arisen in any systems or structures that you are creating.

If you are unsure of your path, you should take your time making a decision; any doubts as to the appropriate path will blow away and progress will be made.

Wealth You are honoured three times in a single day.

Gifts and favours are bestowed upon you.

Your project will reach a high level of success. There is profit from the undertaking.

Relationships Behaving in an angry aggressive way is not really the way to get things done and keep people on side. You want or expect to progress independently but this is not intended; there are not the means or expected conditions. But people will help; a fellow traveller sees your light and helps you. A female ancestor or a living female relative also assists your endeavours.

Marriage and relationships experience harmony and prosperity.

Travel brings progress. Long-distance travel is possible and successful.

Marketplace A new business will prosper. Business in general will increase and grow. Successful business alliances are formed.

Be exceptionally wary of dubious, unethical practices of any kind. People are hiding things away and acquiring things in an unethical manner. These practices will lead to a very serious situation and a splitting apart.

It is a good time for horse fairs and the horse industry.

If looking for work, you will find it. If you are already employed, you will be promoted.

At school or university, students will win recognition.

Feng shui *Jin* advises the care and maintenance of your own 'city walls' (they could be decayed or cracking).

36 Ming Yi 明夷

Together, the characters **Ming Yi** mean brightness obscured or exterminated. **Ming's** components are **Jie**: sun; and **Yue**: moon. **Yi** means raze, exterminate, wipe out. **Yi's** components are **Ren**, meaning man; and the **radical** for bow.

Image Show your intelligence by not showing your intelligence.

In the field In ancient times the evil tyrant Chou captured King Wen. King Wen avoided death by feigning madness. The evil Chou thought King Wen not worth killing and imprisoned him instead in a courtyard compound with very high walls where the only things King Wen could see were the tops of some trees and the sky. King Wen used the time to study the stars and their relationship to current weather and agricultural conditions. King Wen then proceeded to update and extend the *I Ching* into the Chinese classical text it now is and on which Dragon Insights are based. King Wen was later rescued by his son and his dynasty ruled China.

Flow Intelligence should be hidden. You see various dubious things going on – stay silent. You should hide your light and knowledge in order to survive the difficulties in your immediate environment. Your knowledge should be kept to yourself; not visible to other people. Activity now will cause more difficulties or make others jealous.

There are many barbarians about; stay out of the firing line, feign insanity if necessary!

This is not a time of going forward or beginning anything new. This situation is a natural condition of the time and not your fault. You should use this time to restore your energy. Wait patiently for the sun to rise again (and it will). Prepare to implement something new or to replace something outmoded.

Wealth on all levels is limited at this time, so use your resources well. In the end the difficulties bring great prosperity. Like King Wen, take advantage of problems and difficult situations rather than be overcome by them.

Don't relinquish your values or ethics in order to attain wealth. You won't go hungry if you stick to your principles (quietly); ordinary people will admire and support you.

Relationships A person of dark nature is in a position of authority and capable of bringing harm to the wise and able person (you or the person enquired about). Keep a low profile and be prudent, cautious and reserved in everything.

Optimistic people think they can change or bring out the best in the person of dark nature. This is not true; the person concerned really does have no good intentions and is not to be depended on. This will be made very clear. There will be no improvement in the situation. Get out of the situation and away from the person.

Ming Yi says be assured that this dark situation will reach a climax. The person of dark nature will rise to the heights of prominence and hold the spotlight for a short time only, before the natural, timely forces of light and goodness rise up and overwhelm that person.

Travel away from the difficulties and the person of dark nature is possible with effort and cunning. Other travel is not likely.

Marketplace This is not the time for business expansion or an advertising campaign. A person is temporarily eclipsed at work by an interloper. Or there could be a hostile company takeover. Carry on quietly at this time; the light of your enterprise will shine again. It is a good time for study and research.

37 Jia Ren 家人

Jia means family, home, dwelling, a person or family engaged in a certain trade, specialist in a certain field, a school of thought, domestic, live in. **Ren** means man, person. Together **Jia Ren** means members of a family, clan, closely knit group, or a group living together.

Image The perseverance of a woman, or persevering like a woman, will benefit you. Use the *yin*, feminine side of your being.

In the field Members of a family or close-knit group or establishment have confidence and majesty because they are all in their proper places, doing tasks suited to them. The woman or person who prepares nourishment is the centre of this family or group. The one who cooks food is the greatest treasure. In lovingly feeding those close by, that person symbolically nourishes the universe and sets it in order.

Flow Words should be seen by example to be true. Words and actions should be consistent. These are the most important two sentences in *Jia Ren* and go to the heart of the matter; actually doing what you say you are going to do or being who you really are.

Establish firm guidelines and boundaries at the beginning of your endeavours, and listen to women's opinions on these matters and on your endeavours in general. Take care of domestic, family affairs or the 'housekeeping' affairs needed to keep your business or group functioning internally before attending to other affairs or, on a more personal note, take care of your inner wellbeing before taking care of external matters.

Love, fair-mindedness and a balanced outlook are the way to control the family or group. Being angry makes people afraid of you. Make demands of yourself first and lead the way with a good example. The outcome and order within the family or enterprise depends on the calibre of the person or people in charge.

Wealth Cash and material wealth increases. There is progress in goals and enterprises.

To be able to prepare food for yourself and others with only love in your heart and the purest of thoughts in your mind leads to infinite wealth in all realms of your being.

Relationships Do not assume separate goals from those around you at this time; work in harmony with them. Complete independence is not a good idea now – why miss out on the love that surrounds you?

Help comes from an influential benefactor.

There is a strong possibility of establishing a new household in a new and better location.

At this time, love and marriage are warm and cosy.

Marketplace Ensure that products or services live up to their advertising.

Cooking in a warm, loving, secure environment or home. Chefs and cooks, especially female, benefit greatly. They may move to a new restaurant or kitchen profitably. Family restaurants prosper. Households are happy.

Feng shui Excellent feng shui for houses, homes and family restaurants.

Miscellaneous In one example, a young male friend received *Jia Ren* when he was wondering about the course of his life and career. He could not really understand the answer in the context of his question – he lived alone and he hated cooking. About one year later this young man found his answer – he realised he was gay and 'came out'.

If you can understand *Jia Ren's* advice in the context of your question, it doesn't necessarily mean you are gay. This story relates to the opening sentences in the 'Flow' section – words and actions being consistent.

38 *Kui* 日癸

The ancient meaning for **Kui** is strange. **Kui's** component characters are **Ri** meaning sun, day, light; **Yao** meaning an early death or to die young; and **Ren** meaning person. In ancient pronunciations the word for ghosts sounded the same as the word for strange, but with a different written character.

Image The spirits of your ancestors help you to avoid mistakes when you are experiencing unusual circumstances. Seeing strange things in strange times.

In the field The hot sun shines strongly over a lake or marsh. This produces steamy, hazy vapours that give everything a dreamlike, unreal quality. Spirits are seen in the day, which is unusual.

Flow *Kui* talks about seeing things clearly, and correctly recognising people and situations correctly with strange hazy qualities. If you see bad and recognise it as such, you can avoid it.

Kui's theme contains strong images of the Daoist concepts of action through non-action. If something is lost, don't run after it. If it is really your own, really part of your essential nature, be it idea or object, it will return to you by itself.

A situation or action may come along that you would like to take part in. This action begins badly, almost embarrassingly. This causes a change of mind and the anticipated action goes no further.

Your opinions may not meet with agreement. Retain your individuality, but a change in attitude or way of looking at something may be to your benefit.

New plans should be put on hold for a while.

Wealth In small matters, there is good fortune. In all facets of life, small things bring success: doing small things, selling small things, creating small things, making small things, buying small things – these are all beneficial.

Relationships You may unexpectedly, in a lane or village street, meet a man who is a friend or acquaintance. Whether there is further involvement with this man depends on your observations of previous dealings with him. Usually there is no further interaction.

You may feel isolated in these strange times, and see strange and wondrous sights. At first you may be afraid, and ready yourself for defence from attack, but there is no need for such action. The person who approaches now is not a thief but someone who seeks a sincere union and to give aid.

The spirits of rain, fertility, matrimony all aid and assist you, but don't rush into any sort of union or partnership right now.

Travel is not likely at this time.

Market place Don't expand business right now, even if things look good – they are not. Small things bring success. General salespersons, minor diplomats and some artists benefit at this time.

Miscellaneous Denise woke up feeling as if she had had a really important dream that she couldn't remember. Denise consulted the Insights every morning and on this day she received *Kui*. A short time later, she realised she couldn't find her house and car keys. Retracing her steps she went out to the back lane to see if she had dropped them there. A male neighbour was standing there, he had just found her keys. After that Denise and her two-year-old son went to a friend's house but her son staged an enormous, uncontrollable tantrum and so she went straight home. Later that afternoon she thought she saw her 83-year-old father standing outside her house waving to her. This was very strange because he lived in another country. She went outside but there was no-one there. At about 6 pm that night, she had a phone call from her brother saying that their father had died peacefully in his sleep that afternoon.

39 Jian

Jian means lame, cripple, feeble, inadequate, unlucky. **Jian** drawn twice means difficulty or trouble. **Jian**'s components are **Zu** meaning foot; and the character for **radical 40** meaning roof. Feet confined underneath a roof are not going to walk far.

Image Attempting to finish something that has been impeded, rather than beginning something new, brings good fortune.

In the field Growth is impeded by too much water. There is difficulty in walking or movement. The farmer's cart, containing produce bound for market, is stuck in the mud. It's not a lucky day for the farmer, but friends and neighbours assist. Eventually the crop makes it to the market.

Flow It is as if there is a mountain behind you that is too rugged to climb, and a raging river that cannot be crossed, barring any advance. You can't go forward and can't go back. It is hard to find which way to go. Be still for a moment and consider; try lateral thinking – go sideways. There is a narrow way between the mountain and the river. Follow this path – eventually you will find a mountain pass or a safe place to cross the river.

Help will be found in the north-west in the southern hemisphere and in the south-west in the northern hemisphere. There are lots of people and a good marketplace in this direction. The north-west (south-west in north hemisphere), as well as being an actual direction in which to go, also represents a place (or state of mind) where things are harvested and completed. The south-east in the southern hemisphere or north-east in the northern hemisphere is not the direction for you at this time. The south-east (north-east in north hemisphere) is the direction where new things are begun. Things that are new, young, or just beginning don't benefit your cause at this time.

If there are difficulties that make it hard to move about, then be still. Persevere inwardly when it is apparent that you must do something that seems to lead away from your goal. Only go forward directly into difficulties and danger if it is your vocation, job or duty.

Wealth The flow of wealth on all levels of your being is temporarily obstructed. Right now your major source of wealth is in your relationships. Being supported by good people, your goals are achieved. The difficulties are temporary and eventually will be a source of good fortune.

Relationships *Jian* says that in times of difficulties, stay where you are situated and appreciate the love and support in your environment. Join with friends of like-mind.

Don't blame others for your difficulties but look for the source of difficulty within yourself. Neither should you go forth into difficulties recklessly, leaving behind people who need your support and who would not fare very well without it.

Finally, *Jian* says when you have surmounted difficulties and left them behind, help others overcome their difficulties.

It is not a good time for love and marriage. A woman will be pursued by two men.

Travel It is not a good time for long-distance travel. Local travel is helpful.

Marketplace Business is temporarily impeded and slow. Now is not the time for new, young, untried enterprises or anything that is just starting. Established, guaranteed, mature enterprises and products benefit.

Matters in government, public or corporate arenas may take longer to conclude than anticipated. The official or public servant you deal with also encounters impediments or obstruction. Nevertheless this person manages to arrive at the outcome you desire.

40 Jie 解

Jie means relieve, loosen, untie, undo, cut apart, opinion, view, explain, understand. **Jie**'s components are **Chio** meaning horn, trumpet; **Nui** meaning cow or ox; and **Dao** meaning knife. Image of a sharp knife made from ox or cow horn used to loosen things and to skin a cow or ox.

Image Deliverance from troubles is coming very soon – ready or not.

In the field Looking at the sky, the farmer knows that it is going to rain very soon, rain desperately needed for the young seedlings' survival. The farmer prepares for the rain by doing all the jobs around the field that should be done to maximise the rain's benefit.

Flow Very soon, something very good, that you've been anticipating hopefully, is going to occur. This good event is going to solve a heap of difficulties and enable you to continue onwards in your endeavours. It is important that you do all the things you said you were going to do while waiting for this event to happen. Otherwise, the benefits from this good event will be impeded because you're not properly prepared. Finish all the outstanding tasks that need to be done. Set your current affairs in order, then return to your regular routine until the good event occurs (which will be soon).

Be self-confident; great things can be achieved. If there is something you have to do in a place you can get to, then go and attend to this matter quickly. Early action will bring good fortune. Begin your activities early in the morning.

The north-western direction in the southern hemisphere (south-western in the northern hemisphere) brings good fortune. There are lots of people there and a good marketplace. The north-west (south-west in north hemisphere), as well as being an actual direction, also represents a place, or state of mind, where things are harvested or completed.

Wealth Somebody comes to your aid. Let them do so without fuss; be thankful. Keep still for awhile, take a few deep breaths, and do some planning. After that you can begin to find riches. Wealth arrives in all realms of your being.

Don't flaunt gains, flash your cash or behave frivolously. Such behaviour attracts robbers, exploitation and bad karma. Behave modestly and stay on the side of the ordinary people.

Relationships Pardon errors and forgive misdemeanours.

A corrupt, highly placed person will be removed when their vulnerabilities are exposed. If you must remove such a cunning person from your field of endeavour, you will gain a central position with the resources needed to shoot straight for your goal.

You find the solutions needed in a time of deliverance, giving people confidence in your ability.

Be aware of your companions. Is there an inner connection with them? If not, untie or loosen yourself from them. Relax alone for awhile. True sincere friends and helpers will come; people with whom great things can be accomplished.

There is good fortune for those about to be married or in any formal type of partnership or union.

There is great happiness at home. Do not fear quarrels.

Travel is an excellent option right now. Ensure that all your affairs are in good order before departure.

Marketplace Business will be marvellous very soon, with great growth and expansion – are you ready for it? You can expect to make a profit. There are lots of potential customers, with a good market for your endeavours in the north-west in the southern hemisphere and the south-west in the northern hemisphere.

Work in the public, or work on public matters, brings good fortune.

A job is found easily. People already working achieve an important position.

Students pass exams.

41 *Sun* 損

Sun means decrease, subtract, harm; damage, shabby, bad luck, loss, disadvantage. **Sun's** components are **Shou**: hand, hold in the hand; **Kou**: mouth; and **Bei**: money. (Hand to mouth money.) Before the Han dynasty **Sun** meant to decrease by pouring away; drawn with **Shou** meaning hand, and **Yuan** meaning a bronze vessel used for sacrificial offerings of liquors. (Hands holding or pouring out the sacrificial wine.)

Image In times of scarcity, smile as you give something away. Then Heaven smiles on you – indeed it is a miracle!

In the field *Sun* pictures ancient China in mid-spring. The peasants have paid their taxes, survived the rigours of winter when nothing could be grown, and splashed out at the Lunar New Year on fancy food, new clothes and presents. After all that, money, supplies and resources were disappearing fast. The peasants tightened their belts and planted out rice seedlings in marshy paddy fields on the mountainside. Every available pair of hands was needed in order to get a large enough crop planted in time. Big building projects or anything that kept the peasants away from the fields was banned.

Flow A loss is temporary. For now, reduce expenses or outgoings and behave simply, with good humour. Having work to do, a direction to take, or a place to go, brings relief.

Wealth Don't try to cover up a deficiency or scarcity; don't be ashamed or embarrassed about it. The wheel of fortune will turn sooner than you think and you will have amazingly good luck. Consulting the Insights ten times in a row would say the same thing. You attract this exceptional good fortune through kindness and a sincere heart.

Relationships When you stop being stubborn, irritable or dwelling on the negative, then you will obtain able helpers. Pour sacrificial wine for the ancestors, make a simple offering with two bowls of rice, then the higher aspects of the soul are enriched. Afterwards two friends can eat and drink the offerings, which have become holy food, *Prashad*.

Help someone else when your own tasks are done. A little bit of selfless service is good, but don't overwhelm people.

A triangle relationship is broken up. The person who is left alone will find the partner intended for them.

A good time to get married. Those already married have harmony.

If someone is sick, send them love, prayers and get well messages. Such actions at this time have the power to strengthen and hearten the sick person and will greatly aid their recovery.

Travel is good if you have a goal or purpose. Keep everything neat, clean and simple. You will reach your destination. If three people travel together, then one person will be left alone. Afterwards that person finds the right companion.

Marketplace Business at this time is not good, but prosperity and increase come later. There is a lot of work to be done, lucrative products are still in production.

Big building projects do not benefit at this time.

It is a good time for study and research.

Employment will be found in areas of production and manufacture.

Miscellaneous Claudia received *Sun* when she was experiencing a severe cash shortage. Bills were mounting up, the fridge was empty and the electricity would be cut off at any time because she didn't have $60 for the extremely overdue bill. She had a job interview but not even the bus fare to get there. So she walked the nine kilometres to the job interview. She got the job and was walking the nine kilometres back home again when a gust of wind blew a pile of rubbish out of the gutter and sent it swirling around her feet. She looked down and there was a $100 bill sticking to the top of her foot! Food, electricity payment, and bus fares to her new job.

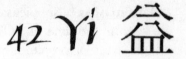

42 Yi 益

Yi means increase, benefit, profit, advantage. **Yi**'s components are **Min**: vessel, dish, earthenware utensils, tiles; and the **radical** for clasp or table, or water. Clasping a dish filled with water.

Image Go for it! Don't hesitate! *Yi* offers control of your life.

In the field A strange and wonderful tree grows, a tree that has abundant foliage and fruit. Some call it the money tree, others see it as the Tree of Life. But the truly wondrous thing about this tree is that it is a topsy-turvy tree, an upside-down tree; foliage and flowers at the bottom and the trunk and roots at the top.

Flow The goal, project, or dream enquired about is the right one to pursue. Heaven blesses your actions and gives assistance so that your endeavours may be completed. Even unfortunate events turn to your advantage. But you must work very hard and use all your energy to complete Heaven's tasks. Go forth! The time is right for successful achievement of great endeavours. But attend to small matters as you go or before you start.

Use the time well; the time of increase does not last as the cycle continues onwards.

Wealth Kindness and sincerity will bring happiness to your door. There will be prosperity in material affairs, and double profit when goals are clear and actions timely. If you have been worried about money, there is some coming. There is money in the bank or waiting somewhere to be collected.

There is a flowering in spiritual matters. Ancient sanskrit scriptures say that the upside-down tree growing in the field represents the impermanent transient nature of the world; worldly objects that are ever-wavering, unsteady and always changing positions; illusionary. Sages say people should try to understand this truth and develop higher vision.

Relationships Wise, pleasant and energetic people of vision are seen in the time of *Yi* helping others. A person who has a high status or profile in the community and who does not help the poor or disadvantaged will be subject to hostility.

An impartial person may become the mediator between two people or groups involved in a dispute. The way to settle this dispute is to seek some compromise from one side and a more generous-hearted approach from the other side, which holds most of the power in this situation.

Whenever or wherever good positive tendencies are observed, you should emulate them. But the source of negative tendencies and habits seen in others should be sought within yourself and removed.

Disagreements are settled. All partnerships and relationships work well, prosper and grow.

A good time to marry. Marriages are harmonious and fruitful, producing children and increasing the family coffers. Good prospects for a new love interest; the person enquired about is a treasure.

Travel is timely and achieves all the desired objectives.

Marketplace All business is profitable and expanding.

Miscellaneous In 1983 I was packing for my spiritual sojourn. At that time I had no idea that I would ever be writing a book about the *I Ching* and therefore decided not to take the Richard Wilhelm thick and scholarly hard-back edition of the *I Ching* with me – it was too heavy for lugging around Asia, I thought. I placed the book on the shelf above my bag and left the room, but when I came back the book was in the bag. I took it out of the bag and put it back on the shelf and left the room but when I returned, the book was in the bag again. This happened three times. The third time I left the book in the bag and did a coin *I Ching* into why I should take the book with me. The answer was *Yi* and it sure was right! Taking the *I Ching* book with me certainly led to a great increase on all levels of my being, with this book as tangible evidence of that.

43 Quai 夬

Quai means decision, resolution; open out, cut off, execute, cleanse; purify, clear out; certainly, undoubtedly. **Quai's** components are **Shui**: water, stream; and **Kuai**: forked; parted.

Image Creative dragons of yang energy grow stronger and stronger within you; awaiting and demanding perfection. Energetic action is required.

In the field *Quai* shows a stream cutting a path for the flow of its waters. A breakthrough. *Quai's* ancient image comes from the fifth solar month (third lunar month in the northern hemisphere), just before the heavy monsoon rains were due. Farmers were instructed to make ready for this rain rather than be flooded out by it, to create channels and irrigation systems.

Flow There is something big and worrisome coming at you. This problem must be faced squarely, and solutions found, before you are overwhelmed by it. Follow the farmer's example and create some channels as outlets and inlets. Decisions must be made or the 'flooding rains' will take and make their own course.

Don't rely on past achievements or work already done to see you through this situation. Previous strategies are not sufficient. This problem needs new improved solutions, hard thinking and energetic work. Do some planning first rather than reacting to the situation with excessive, aggressive, premature action. Do one thing at a time. Stay within your limits. Don't change work that has been already done.

Quai says that once overly abundant things in your environment – the weeds, obstacles or negative traits – have been removed, you must be constantly on the lookout for their reappearance and ready for their instant removal.

Wealth You can achieve success in your endeavours and

acquire riches, happiness and honour. Don't hoard things at this time; generous giving in thought, word and deed as you accumulate will be beneficial.

At this time your mind may be unsettled and agitated, making it hard to focus. The solution is to meditate on and follow the ways of a holy person. *Quai* comments that most people are not interested in doing this but Heavenly nourishment is definitely available to strengthen your powers of concentration and aid spiritual development. You may meet a heavenly dragon in the breath of meditation.

Sickness disappears.

Relationships Don't be afraid to speak openly and truthfully about the problem to people in authority or in an open forum where everybody who needs to can hear. Communicate with all parties involved in the situation so that intelligent decisions can be made. Accept good advice wherever it is found.

All types of partnerships are tense right now; people are competitive and argumentative. Selfless service to others will benefit you.

Do not go to war (metaphorically, metaphysically or literally).

Travel brings relief from tension.

Marketplace There is increasing profit in a growing market, but the competition is aggressive. Your enterprise will need some smart new strategies to maintain its position. Don't use advertising, promotions or any avenues of action used before in this situation or a similar one; something new and original is needed. Don't put all your eggs in one basket – try a variety of strategies and promotions in a variety of areas. Create tributaries and channels all through your 'field'. Organising a business credit facility to keep cash flowing evenly is a good idea. Be generous to employees to ensure loyalty.

Literature is in the limelight; writing benefits.

All aspects of the silk industry benefit.

Those who seek employment with the government or in an official capacity are successful.

People pass important exams and tests.

Fish, fishing and the fishing industry benefit.

Clear all channels – internal and external.

Feng shui Attend to the roof of a house/building. Inspect all water courses. Repair river, lake and dam banks if necessary. Unblock all drains.

Miscellaneous Paul had lived in Kathmandu for two years. He had originally travelled there solely to get stoned, but he met a Buddhist monk who became his spiritual teacher. Paul gave up his indulgences and went to live with his teacher far away in the mountains at a Buddhist temple. He had been writing some short stories about his experiences with the idea of acquiring enough material for a book.

Paul had to return to Kathmandu when he ran out of moeny. His yearly resident foreigner's visa was expiring in three weeks and he needed US$2,000 to renew it. The authorities get clamp down on foreigners without visas. He consulted the Insights and drew *Quai*. He understood the part about the weeds growing back because since arriving back in Kathmandu he had been tempted by old indulgences again.

Paul spent most of his remaining money on Nepalese handicrafts and posters and sent them to a friend with a shop in Germany. Then he sent his short stories to publications all over the USA. Then, putting all his trust in the Buddha's teachings, Paul humbly went to the visa office two weeks before his visa expired. He spoke to the supervisor there, truthfully explaining his situation. It so happened that that supervisor knew his teacher and gave Paul a free two-month visa extension. Paul made just enough money from the craft sales in Germany to pay for his visa renewal. Then, slowly his stories began to sell. As far as I know, he is still meditating on that faraway mountain in Nepal.

44 Gou 女后

Gou means pair; copulate; good. **Gou's** components are **Nu**: girl, woman, female; **Hou**: queen, empress, ruler; and **K'ou**: mouth, entrance, opening, hole, gorge, a pass, port. **Gou** pictures a woman, a queen or empress; a female ruler issuing orders through entrances, openings, gorges, a pass, port.

Image A female (leader or ruler) makes her first appearance and communicates her intentions and instructions.

In the field *Gou* talks about the conditions of the seventh solar month when the male, yang, creative energy of summer has reached its peak. The female, yin, receptive energy of winter first appears and begins its natural (cyclic) takeover. In ancient times, officials met to discuss the coming winter and to send edicts, communications and requests for supplies to areas that became inaccessible once the snow set in. They communicated about the protection, maintenance and accessibility of entrances to cities and provinces, and about keeping the routes used for communication and trade (gorges, passes and harbours) open through the winter.

Flow Illusions abound during this time. There is a tendency for you to ignore potentially dangerous people or things (including germs and ideas) when they first appear because they seem to be insignificant and harmless. A simple example of this is one little weed appearing in the garden. The gardener thinks 'It's just one little weed. It can't do much damage, I'll pull it out later.' Next time the gardener looks, that one little weed has set seed and is spreading throughout the garden. If the weed had been pulled out straight away, it could never have gained influence and become harmful.

Wealth If your endeavours are in harmony with the will of Heaven, achievement and wealth on all levels of your being comes like ripe fruit dropping from a tree. You find 'hidden chapters, essays and music'. You may find your life work. It is a wondrous, creative time.

The power of the moon is rising. The moon is the symbol of the mind, the intellect, the *buddhi*. If the mind can be kept on track at this time, not dazzled by 'moonlight reflections sparkling on the water', great spiritual progress can be made.

Relationships This is the proper and natural time of the female yin coming to meet the male yang. This is the time for pairing, meeting, encountering, and communicating; having social and sexual intercourse.

Pregnancy is very possible at this time.

There is peace in the family.

Travel It is a good time for travelling, but be wary of the potentially dangerous people and things mentioned in the flow. Meeting a friend far from home increases the traveller's good fortune daily.

Marketplace Make sure your communication systems are adequate and make sure that you use them to a maximum.

All aspects and areas of the communication industry prosper and benefit.

Public speaking comes easily at this time.

Writers will experience good fortune.

It is good time for short-term and seasonal business.

Entertainment enterprises will be profitable.

Tuning, adjusting and repairing musical instruments is beneficial.

Levying or increasing fees and taxes in the marketplace doesn't benefit at this time.

Attend to fire hazards in your environment.

Feng shui If you see a little problem in the property enquired about, there is a big problem right behind it. Have a trades-person check the property thoroughly. This could also be a problem with the finance, contract or agent for the property.

45 Cui 萃

Cui means gather together, assemble; gathering of people, collection of things. **Cui**'s components are **Cao**: grass, flowers; and **Zu**: follower. Followers with flowers (in their hair).

Image Gathering lots of things or people together in one place requires organisation.

In the field In ancient times, a crowd of people gathered beside a lake on a mountain near a temple for the summer solstice ceremony. The Emperor, who was to lead the ceremony, prepared himself by fasting and meditating in order to communicate with God and spirits.

Flow *Cui* talks about event organisation and coordination. It describes various people and processes involved in gathering together. A central location and theme for gathering together is important. At the beginning, consult a recognised person or official in authority who is skilled in the matter enquired about, someone who thoroughly understands all the requirements needed for your gathering together. Then what you seek is obtained and enterprises are accomplished.

Work for the benefit of the whole event. Consider everybody's requirements, not your personal gain. Your work will then be crowned with success.

Wealth You will achieve endeavours and find the wealth you seek. The gate of unhappiness closes and the gate of happiness opens. The peach tree blossoms – happy events follow in succession.

Sickness disappears.

Relationships Don't try to pre-empt events. Heaven is at work ensuring that those who belong together at the gathering are brought together.

There will always be someone in the group who is not happy with the way things are being organised, who finds fault at every turn. This old stick-in-the-mud-grump needs a stimulating, uplifting and motivational pep talk.

Another person is isolated and discouraged at the edge of the group, far from the action. This person should advance towards the middle of the gathering by getting close to the associates of the leaders.

Lastly there is the individual driven to tears and distress because the person they want to align themselves with misunderstands and mistrusts them. This distress makes the other understand that the individual's intentions are true.

Attend a large event or family gathering.

Travel in general is rewarding. You gain a great deal of understanding about your relatives or group. A business buying trip will be successful and lucrative. A large group of people travelling together may experience some hitches and confusion on their journey but they have some fun along the way and eventually reach their destination.

Marketplace It is a very busy and prosperous marketplace. A big opening or launch for your product or enterprise reaps a fortune.

Clearly signposted directions to an event will be beneficial.

Be ready for unscheduled occurrences during the time of *Cui*. When many people gather together, there will be the possibility of arguments and fights. When great possessions or things of value are accumulated in one place, theft is likely. Guard against the possibilities. Insurance policies and security precautions benefit.

Event coordinators and venues prosper.

Scholars pass exams with honours.

Feng shui Consider the placement of doors and entrances. Perhaps the current main entrance should be closed off and another entrance used as the main entrance or a new entrance created.

46 Sheng 升

Sheng means ascend, rise, elevate, promote; a standard measurement; peaceful, calm. In classical mandarin, **Jie** meaning sun appears above **Sheng**. The sun making things ascend and grow; photosynthesis. Alternatively, **Sheng** appears with **Yi**: city or district; and **Tu**: earth. Measuring inside the city. Ascending the city wall.

Image A direct, vertical ascent from obscurity to recognition, from seedling to abundant growth. Many small things are done to build up something great and high.

In the field *Sheng*'s image shows the time between the monsoon season and the harvest market. In the monsoon season, the rain poured down; then the sun shone brightly, giving crops the power to grow rapidly. Suddenly crops were tall and abundant, soon to be ready for the marketplace. Meanwhile, in the city, officials prepared for the harvest market crowds. Measuring devices and weights were checked and put in order. Marketplace regulations were standardised.

Flow Don't be afraid to speak with the necessary people in authority concerning your endeavours; Heaven favours them and will assist you. But the time for action is now so get moving! Success for your activities will be found in a northerly direction in the southern hemisphere or a southerly direction in the northern hemisphere. This direction also signifies a place or a state of mind, where things are ready for harvesting.

Don't let early successes go to your head. Proceed step by step; don't skip anything. Goals will be achieved and an abiding course is found, but good fortune should not be overplayed. Don't lose touch with reality and ordinary people when endeavours have reached the peak of their success – take a break. Ascending without rest leads to exhaustion. Know when to stop, know when to harvest.

Wealth All strong desires will be fulfilled, your wealth on all levels will grow rapidly. Be adaptable along the way, focusing on final outcomes.

An idea for creating new wealth is a good one. A person in authority agrees and will support or sponsor this endeavour. This creates the confidence to express yourself, then you grow and blossom.

Matters concerning wealth in any realm of your being proceed with such great ease and good fortune that it is almost scary. Don't waste this precious time and mind space worrying about how long this unobstructed, positive, forward movement will last – just milk this good fortune for all it's worth while you have it.

Relationships *Sheng* talks about a person who is an honest straight talker; some people don't appreciate these qualities. But this person is upright and on the side of ordinary people and ensures the rules and measures are the same for all.

At home, peace reigns and all relationships are good. This is a good time to formalise or endorse all types of unions and partnerships. A new love interest is an honourable, reliable good soul.

Missing persons are found.

Travel Travellers will make contact. Travel is everything you hoped for.

Marketplace It is time to do the many small jobs needed to get your product or enterprise into a very busy lucrative marketplace, where it will be a best-seller.

Help comes from people in authority.

Small things bring success.

Franchising benefits.

Creative people sell their wares for an excellent price and become well known.

There are plenty of good employment opportunities available in your field.

A well-earned promotion will come along for those already employed.

In business and finance, hold out for the highest bid.

47 *Kun* 困

Kun means stranded, hard-pressed, confined, exhausted, distressed; lay siege to, surround, pin down. **Kun**'s components are the **radical** for enclosure; and **Mu**: tree. A tree in an enclosure.

Image Don't bother speaking. Save your breath, though your words are true, you are not believed.

In the field Movement and growth in the field are stunted. The water level in the lake or paddy field is very low. There is an oppressive regime in power and resources are frugal. The farmer is weary and worried.

Flow Everybody experiences *Kun* at some time – it is a natural part of the cycle and will pass. *Kun* could simply be saying you are too tired and your thoughts aren't clear. Perhaps, instead of reading INSIGHTs, you should be resting both body and brain. Or perhaps you have asked too many questions in a row.

Your everyday life may be in satisfactory order, but you have dreams and goals itching to be achieved and you feel trapped. Don't try forcibly to remove the oppression; meditate on the matter and prepare.

Kun says when you are depressed by life's events, don't fall into a dark mood, feeling sorry for yourself and dwelling on the negative – Heaven does knows what it is doing. Do something pleasant and soothing that takes your mind off your worries.

Someone looking for able helpers comes to assist but you may be so caught up in oppression that when conditions change for the better, you do not believe in the changes and are afraid to make a move. Make a start and be amazed.

Wealth and energy on all levels is very low. Highly placed (government) people see aid is needed and want to help, but are obstructed from action by their peers. The obstruction is temporary; a rescue package will be put together. A (government) helper arrives after a time. Things slowly come right. For now, be prudent in everything you do. Limit your alcohol intake to avoid any stomach trouble. Spiritual endeavours, research, study and seclusion lead to a wealth of knowledge and a source of wealth.

Relationships A mean person tries to fool you. There are tricky people about; you see them, but others don't. Do not speak about them; it is of no use. Even though what you say is true, no one will believe it, but Heaven will console and aid you. Do not be afraid to stand alone – quietly alone.

Sometimes you are suffering so much mental (self-inflicted) pain that you spurn those closest to you; those who want to give comfort to ease that suffering. By such action others are hurt and withdraw their support and you become isolated.

Don't carry conflicts through to the end; compromise and get free of the situation. Avoid criminals and dubious characters.

Joining with friends is good but too much alcohol is not.

The object of your affections is married or good as married.

Travel is really not a good option right now.

Marketplace Material and commercial endeavours will not succeed at this time.

Business does not thrive; the marketplace is too restrictive. Nobody has any money. New partnerships do not thrive.

Feng shui This building has problems with drainage.

In winter or heavy rain the ground is swampy and marsh-like.

48 Jing 丼

Jing means a well, a deep pit, a shaft; 22nd of the 28 lunar constellations; neat, orderly.

Image A Well of Knowledge. An external ordering of your life will not bring happiness; find the internal source of your life. Look for the well of knowledge within yourself.

In the field The character *Jing* is drawn to represent eight fields surrounding a central field containing the well. In ancient times the people from the surrounding eight fields shared the well. Together they cultivated the central field and the produce from it was given to the landowner or king, for rent or taxes. An entire city can be moved but not its source of water.

Flow If you have been obstructed in a particular endeavour that you have set your mind on, be patient; this delay is to the good. When the obstructions to action are removed (and they will be – even if it takes a year), your path will be smoother than you ever thought possible.

Wealth A well that is in good order serves everyone and never runs dry. The well must be maintained if people are to continue drinking the water from it. *Jing* says a well is like knowledge or talent – it must be used to stay healthy. If a person has good qualities and a fine mind but does not utilise them, these qualities will erode and crack. Then, such a person accomplishes nothing.

If any part of your life or being is not prospering, this can be fixed. Wealth is available in all realms. You need to energise yourself, develop some new strategies for endeavours; revamp and update; rethink the way you have been approaching things and people. At this time your mind is very clear and lucid; the new improved version of your endeavours will become more and more brilliant. The new, improved version has the assurance of blessings from Heaven and a lot of money as well.

Relationships An able person is available to help in your endeavours. This person is not well known; only his/her friends know how talented this person is. Send a request for help to the universe, then look around and ask questions. You will find the person that you seek.

Marriage will be enduring and prosperous. All types of new unions and partnerships will flourish, as long as people do not take each other for granted. Like the well, relationships have to be maintained and taken care of.

Encourage people to try to find common ground or a central theme that will draw them all together to assist each other.

Travel Moving to another location or travelling for career, study, business, family or relationship commitments will be a success. But sometimes there is no need to move or travel. The thing or source that you need or seek is there inside yourself or within your present environment.

Marketplace The gushing of a new well or endeavour increases happiness and prosperity. This well is centrally located – people can come and go easily.

New endeavours, enterprises, projects and investments benefit.

Cattle, sheep and horse industries prosper.

The building and construction industry benefits at this time, as does the silk industry.

Students pass examinations.

Putting your work aside will not benefit you.

Feng shui A moving water feature improves your fortunes at this time, particularly in the shape of a well, but a fountain would be fine; big or small, indoor or outdoor, it does not matter. Place it in a north-east area in the southern hemisphere or a south-east area in the northern hemisphere.

Miscellaneous *I Ching* refers to itself as a well; there for all, anyone can use it. No matter how many people come, they will all find what they need.

49 Ge 革

Ge means change, transform, renew, reform, hides, leather, defensive armour; a wing.

Image Deep and profound transformations are possible and bring supreme success. But even small changes for the good bring blessings.

In the field The revolutions of the stars, the seasons and the calendar are observed from the Summer Solstice to the end of autumn when great transformations are seen in the Heavens, the weather, the landscape, the people, and activities. Time for a change.

Flow What has been enquired about has the power to transform your life. Your intentions should be true to your heart and soul; changes you really want or need to happen. The beginning of transformation will be difficult. Therefore the agenda for the matter enquired about should be organised thoroughly. Make a plan to help you achieve your endeavours. A diary might be handy; a calendar is definitely needed. Then confidently make the changes and begin the transformation.

Wealth When transformation is thoroughly undertaken everything responds to your wishes. Intuitively you know exactly what to do. Melancholy disappears and joy comes. The search for wealth on all levels succeeds.

Find out from a Chinese astrologer or Chinese Almanac, the 'stem' and 'branch' of your birthday. Any day containing these two characters will be a good day for you and your endeavours.

Tummy upsets are possible, but there is no serious illness. Plain vegetarian food without strong flavours is beneficial.

Relationships Discuss any changes in detail with all those involved three times, and knot out as many problems as possible before undertaking any changes.

Successful transformations need to be clearly visible to others. A change that cannot be seen and noted by others is not enough. To achieve success in your endeavours, you must dress, think and act as you intend to once your endeavours are achieved. Then you must advertise your endeavours.

A change in your personal life, in all types of relationships and partnerships, is possible and beneficial.

Letters come from far away.

There is nothing to fear from lawsuits.

Travel Travelling changes your point of view and possibly your perception of life.

All travellers find what they are looking for.

Marketplace The marketplace is thriving. It is a good time to change packaging, displays, uniforms or products. Change is beneficial everywhere: government, business, organisation of systems, and job descriptions. Expect a change in career or location.

The textile industry benefits and prospers, especially woven, knitted and winter materials.

All types of street theatre benefit and create more prosperity. Actors and people who are transformed by costume will benefit and prosper.

Well-made metal objects are a good investment.

Miscellaneous The previous insight, #48 *Jing*, suggested looking inward to find the well of knowledge within yourself. The next insight, #50 *Ding*, is where great spiritual and creative gifts are transmitted via a metal sacrificial vessel. The metal for the sacrificial vessel was found in the water from the well of knowledge and now it is being heated, pounded and shaped into a vessel suitable for spiritual food. #49 *Ge* is the transformation process between *Jing* and *Ding*; a very mystical trio indeed. Read *Jing* and *Ding* also to get an idea of the flow of things.

50 Ding 鼎

Ding means an ancient ceremonial tripod used for food; a cauldron with two loop handles. **Ding** is a very ancient character evolving from the use of clay cooking pots in the Neolithic age; a very special and important character in the Chinese psyche. In ancient times, the character **Ding** was interchangeable with the character **Zhen**, meaning to divine, divination.

Image A sacrificial vessel. Supreme good fortune.

In the field In ancient times, The Emperor, the Son of Heaven, made an offering to his ancestors and sought communications with his celestial father, the Emperor of Heaven. He presented fragrant food in a *Ding* with golden handles and jade rings. Insights were interpreted and knowledge transmitted.

Flow Before a *Ding* can be used for offerings or new endeavours, it has to be thoroughly cleaned out to remove any old residue, then polished till it is shiny and bright, ready to receive fresh nourishment and great possessions. You may find yourself getting rid of a lot of bad karma very quickly at this time and generally getting rid of a lot of rubbish, on and in all realms of your being and life. You may have to clean up a self-inflicted mess, but that's OK. It is a good time to cleanse your body of toxins and try to reduce unhealthy habits as well.

For a while, certain rules may curtail your activities and block your way. It seems you will have no fame, fortune or following; nobody seems to notice you much; there are few people to have dialogue with. Keep the faith and hold to the path; rain will fall. Blessings from Heaven will smooth all obstruction and tension away. Mistakes and errors of the past will go. Everything will become favourable; you are in harmony with the will of Heaven.

Wealth Your ears are quick at hearing, your eyes are clear and bright. There is nourishment in all realms: physical, mental, spiritual, and material. Your work finds favour with Heaven, which dispenses great abundance and wealth. You can attain a state of mind in which a divine flow (of knowledge) can be achieved. It is a very good creative period for writing, study or art work, a time when imagination is more powerful than knowledge.

You can make a double profit by possibly winning a prize or award.

Relationships Got something new, shiny and bright? Everyone will want it, better keep it out of sight. Don't be too vocal or showy about the subject of your enquiry. Keep things to yourself as much as possible, otherwise you will encounter jealousy and obstructions. Wait until something is actually finished before advertising or presenting it. When the time comes to find a capable helper, you need to be approachable and modest about your skills, then you attract the right person and everybody prospers. If disagreements pop up, settle them quickly and don't dwell on them.

If enquiring about a new relationship, you have found a soul mate.

Marriage is successful.

Those who have disappeared return.

Travel It is not useful to leave your usual environment(s).

Marketplace A profitable business is established.

Get rid of rubbish, clean out old stock, files and outmoded ideas. Give your enterprise a thorough housecleaning.

There is success and promotion for working people.

Three people are able to work together harmoniously.

There are work opportunities for the unemployed.

Written efforts bring big increases in knowledge and prosperity.

Students will pass exams with recognition.

Farmers and rural people will gain more land.

51 Zhen 震

Zhen means terror, fear, trembling, shaking, vibrate, shock, agitate, move. **Zhen**'s components are **Yu**: rain; and **Chen**: day, star, time, morning.

Image Thunder shakes and vibrates. Great success!

In the field It is time for rain, morning rain, spring rain. The Green Dragon of the East, the Rain Dragon, is over the fields. Everything is shaken into creative action. New life force is set in motion. Seedlings and new, young things vibrate and grow; great changes are taking place.

In the field *Zhen* is about having the faith to walk the Dao, the middle way, amid crashing thunder and lightning bolts; to walk amidst fear, so calmly full of faith, that not one drop of wine is spilt from the sacrificial chalice being carried.

The first shock gives you a big fright. You imagine you are in a much worse situation than anyone else around. Soon you laugh again as the situation becomes clear and to your advantage.

Sometimes a big fright at the start of an endeavour is exactly what is needed for a kick-start; it gets the adrenalin pumping, making you think and act quickly and carefully; making change and moving forward.

But if the shock leaves you stunned and incapacitated, then you are in trouble. The only thing to do is keep a mental picture of whatever or whoever you hold sacred and true, then nothing can harm you. This, of course, takes practice and the deepest faith of all, the faith that Heaven will replenish and energise you with divine love.

Consider Agmogsiddhi, the Green Buddha of the Eastern direction; he personifies the heart and soul of Zhen. He embodies fearless movement, and faith in the certainty that nothing can happen to us that does not belong to us in our innermost being; this is the foundation of fearlessness. Don't lose faith when shock comes. It is true that God works in mysterious ways.

Wealth All types of wealth make a return. After ups and downs and some tense moments, eventually you will be laughing all the way to the bank.

If something is lost, don't waste time and energy trying to get it back. In seven days it returns. Quieten the heart, take deep breaths, and meditate if possible. Faith is needed to take action through non-action. Danger and (quite a big) loss are short term. The secret is to find the balance and stay in the centre of movement.

Relationships Understand the difference between fear and a gut feeling that something is wrong – have faith in yourself. If you have planned to do something, but now have a gut feeling that you shouldn't be doing it, then don't do it, even though it might upset others.

Travel is exciting, thrilling and successful.

Marketplace There is great success for all business in general. New, young or innovative products benefit. It is a good time to begin an enterprise in a new place.

Job opportunities and career advancement will be found without difficulty.

There is good fortune in theatre, broadcasting, sports or the military.

All shades of the colour green are very significant at this time and may feature strongly in some aspect of your life, dress or decor.

Miscellaneous A father of an 18-year-old boy, who had been behaving very badly for some time, received *Zhen* after his son had been arrested. Everyone was frightened and in astate of shock. The son had never been in trouble with the police befroe and had committed only a very minor offence, which ony warranted a caution in court. But the episode was a wake-up call to the young man, who found a full-time job the next day and later went on to university.

52 Gen 艮

The modern meaning of **Gen** is difficult or stubborn, blunt, straightforward, forthright. In ancient times **Gen**'s image was used in the calendar to represent the cold, snowy conditions of winter, when it was best to stay inside; in those times **Gen** meant to stop, to be still.

Image The energy of #51 *Zhen* has been harnessed. The ending and beginning of movement. Power comes from being still.

In the field *Gen*'s image is of spiritual pursuits; sacred mountains and ascetics in caves. *Gen* is the place in legend and ancient teachings where *Shiva* dances, Milaprepa sings, Magic Monkey is born, Vishnu awakes, Wen Shu, Lord of Wisdom is seen, and a 1,000-petalled golden lotus blooms in the Purple Hall of the City of Jade.

Flow Now is the time to stop and be still. You should be so still, within and without, that you neither see nor hear anyone or anything around you, allowing movement and activity to develop naturally. Use deep rhythmic breathing, concentration or relaxation methods and meditation to achieve greater levels of awareness.

This isn't the time for thinking of what might have been or what might occur in the future. It is time to centre thoughts on the here and now. Here and now it is best to still the mind and stop thinking for awhile. Take a moment freed of space and time.

Gen describes the various stages of stilling your body in readiness for meditation. First sit with a straight back. Begin deep, rhythmic breathing and still the toes and feet. Next, still the calves and legs, followed by the pelvic region – this area is difficult to still. Then the trunk of the body – stilling this area brings great peace. After that, still the jawbone, face and head. Finally stillness of the body is achieved and you are ready for meditation.

Wealth The Great Spirit of the Mountain calls: 'I love you very much; wish for anything and I will give it to you.' Who is the one the Great Spirit of the Mountain loves so very much? Someone of fearless, selfless spirit, who can control physical sensations. Where is such a person found? Within yourself. Within the breath.

Are you able to have a little room where you can close the door and be alone? Then that is your cave; that is your sacred mountain; that is your wealth.

Relationships Stilling yourself doesn't necessarily mean being able to stop others from surging forward and falling over their feet. Work alone on endeavours; another person's help will not eventuate.

Visitors will not come, even if they are expected.

Be careful of what you say, and don't say anything about matters that don't concern you directly.

It is not good for new partnerships of any kind right now, but there is harmony for people already married or living together.

Travel Travelling to a faraway place for work will make you prosperous. Travel to a retreat or holy place is beneficial. But the best place to travel right now is inside yourself.

Marketplace Be cautious and prudent in all worldly and material matters right now. Review business strategies and past performance then make a new business plan. Have patience – your ideas are good but the time isn't. Success will come bit by bit.

There is promotion or improved new employment.

Academics receive recognition.

Yoga, meditation and other spiritual institutes and related enterprises will benefit you.

Miscellaneous Pay attention to signs in your body.

53 Jian 漸

Jian means to glide, advance, flow, penetrate, reach; gradually, little by little. **Jian**'s components are **Shui**: water; **Che**: vehicle; and **Ren**: person.

Image Gradual development. Movement without extremes. A tree grows slow and strong on the mountainside.

In the field In ancient times, sages noted the migratory patterns of birds when compiling weather reports. They used feathers in devices for measuring wind. *Jian* pictures wild geese on their annual flight north to Mongolia, gradually gliding and advancing from the shoreline to the rocks, then to dry land, then up to the trees and onwards to the hills and finally to the mountain summit, where their dropped feathers are collected by shamen and used in a sacred dance. There are a few flightpath difficulties for the geese along the way but ultimately great success.

Flow The subject enquired about will have good fortune if its development is allowed to take its proper or natural course. This is not a short-term enterprise. Rather, it is like planting an enormous tree as a seedling; it is going to take a long time to grow to full maturity. Don't apply any force or pressure. Careful, unhurried, constant work returns great profit in the end.

Overconfidence, trying to rush things or impulsive action is not wise. Advancing too far, too fast, without proper formal agreements, will unexpectedly land you in a situation, space or place where there is a strong possibility of theft and where it is hard enough for you just to survive, let alone thrive.

Gradually conditions change. You reach the summit of your endeavours. It is a high, lonely place. You must work very, very hard amid some jealously and slander. But in the end your light is seen and none can deny it. Freed from all difficulties, your glory will shine. Emerge to a brilliant future!

Wealth At the start, there is shelter and the resources needed to carry on, then a path of advance and activity opens up. Wealth on all levels increases slowly, but surely, from a strong solid foundation to long-lasting abundance.

Relationships Advance towards a union. The subject enquired about may meet with gossip and criticism but this does no harm. People who think the same way as you do will come of their own accord.

During the time of *Jian*, you may find yourself temporarily nesting in the wrong tree with some hostile and strange birds for company, like a wild goose perching on the tip of a branch; a tricky situation requiring dexterity and a delicate state of balance. Retreat inwardly if you cannot fly away outwardly. At least this is a safe place where you can hang on.

After you have achieved your success, people will regard you as a shining example to motivate them onwards in their own endeavours.

It is a time of good fortune for love and upcoming marriage. If you are already married, beware a person interested in your spouse.

Be patient with the person you wish to be your partner. If that person is unsure at this time about making a commitment to you, don't try to force things. As it says in the 'Flow', this relationship will not be short term; it will take a long time to mature.

Travel All journeys are successful and fairly smooth. Long journeys should be broken up into easy stages.

Marketplace One hundred per cent profit can be expected from business endeavours.

Contracts pertaining to a union are drawn up.

Formal applications take place.

There are no lawsuits.

It is an excellent time for literary or artistic efforts.

54 Gui Mei 歸妹

Mei means the younger sister. **Gui** means marries. The younger sister marries.

Image The concubine. The mistress, not the wife.

In the field *Gui Mei* pictures a young girl taken into a family as a concubine with no power and very few rights.

Flow Somebody becomes entangled in a powerless, inferior position in a group or family. *Gui Mei* is a definite warning about a person or situation you have recently encountered or will encounter very soon. It is a strong, dangerous force. Sometimes *Gui Mei* may override the question asked if this hazardous situation is unexpectedly imminent. No matter what has been enquired about, this is not the time for it. Best to lay low for awhile – undertakings will bring misfortune.

Fate and karma lead you to a crossroads – don't get run over. Decisions, choices and paths taken at this time can cause serious, arduous detours in your life journey and Heaven's intended outcomes for you.

You may read *Gui Mei* and think 'what a lot of rubbish'. But there are things in this situation that are being kept secret. Hidden agendas and deception abound. Everything concerning this person or situation is an illusion. Listen to what people who are in the know, or associates of the person or situation, say. They are telling the truth about this matter, much as you may not want to acknowledge it as truth.

If already involved in this situation, then extreme caution and reserve are needed. Outward acceptance of this subordinate position will bring relief from immediate tension. Your true glory cannot be hidden even in a lowly, subordinate position. Eventually you find a way out of this dilemma and are rewarded for fortitude and virtue.

Wealth Economy in your personal life is not a mistake.

Think about the transitory nature of all life. Understand that all things will pass. Spiritual endeavours are the only beneficial endeavours at this time. Behaving like a hermit or recluse is in harmony with the times. The matters eluded to in *Gui Mei* can be of such a serious nature that they need a deep and serious approach to finding a solution. An *I Ching* done with coins or yarrow stalks will give you a much more detailed answer and show a way to fearless improvement in your situation. Consult the bibliography at the back of this book for a list of traditional *I Ching* books which will show you how to consult the *I Ching* with coins or yarrow, or consult a *feng shui* practitioner.

Relationships This is not the time for donning your finest feathers or displaying your talents. The wrong people will be attracted. Best to keep a low profile. Romantic, flirting attention you may encounter soon is hazardous, to say the least. If you have enquired about a recent love interest, run away from this person as fast as possible. *Gui Mei* talks about being left with nothing but loneliness and emptiness.

If asking about a man, there is a 99.9 per cent chance he is married or as good as married. He is also a liar and a cheat. *Gui Mei* pictures a naive woman being swept off her feet by an older man, who is not faithful. Heartbreak will follow.

Travel It is not an unreasonable over-reaction to leave the town or country to avoid or escape entanglement in this situation.

Marketplace Be prudent in business transactions, don't buy right now unless necessary. Double-check all calculations. It is not the time to expand, introduce new products or run an advertising campaign.

Don't go into business with a partner.

If you must take the job enquired about, find another new job as soon as possible.

Miscellaneous In answer to a yes/no or should I/shouldn't I type question, the answer is 'no', you should not.

55 Feng 豐

Feng means abundant, plentiful, luxuriant, fruitful. Feng's
components are **Tou**: sacrificial vessel, legumes, a dry measure,
small weight; **Feng**: fine-looking, monument; and **Shan**: mountain.

Image Abundance, greatness, brilliance, prosperity. Great
success!

In the field *Feng* pictures the time around the Summer
Solstice. In ancient times, the Summer Solstice was an important observation point for astronomers, as an indicator of the
intensity and severity of the coming winter. At this time the
crops and foliage have grown to abundant perfection. The
peak of creative energy and power is attained. It is time to
harvest.

Flow *Feng* notes the movement of energy as it begins its
transformation from the creative energy of summer and youth
to the receptive, yin energy of winter and maturity.
Observing, acknowledging and accepting the change in
energy flows is the way to maintain abundance. *Feng*
encompasses the idea of going beyond the normal limits of
vision and thinking to achieve the desired results.

Go forth confidently and meet the person you feel you
should meet with, or do the thing you feel you must do, but
do it quickly and efficiently within a period of 10 days, then
there will be esteem.

Wealth Blessing and fame are nearing. Your reputation grows
as you bring about a state of abundance. But like the sun,
which must begin a natural downward movement towards
sunset once it reaches noon, this abundant state of affairs
reaches its peak, evens out, and will begin a slow decline.
Don't be sad about this – the sun and abundance will rise
again. Behave like the king when he makes offerings at
midday on the Summer Solstice – thankful and confident.

Meanwhile you will be more than adequately affluent and have everything you need.

The sick improve.

Relationships Your vision of how things should be, or will occur, is correct and leads to good fortune. But go slowly putting forth these ideas, and allow people to absorb them little by little, rather than be overwhelmed by them.

You understand the real intentions of some people in your field or work, but the 'emperor' of your field, or your boss, does not. It does no good to speak of it. For a short time, your light is darkened by supercilious minor celebrities in your field of endeavour.

Then people of brilliant ability appear; great luminaries in your field, who suggest the correct strategies for successful action. After that, utilise helpers to the maximum for rewarding results.

Your social life will be very busy. Mature-aged persons are honoured.

There is good luck in love. Long-term relationships and marriages are happy.

Travel Journeys are profitable.

Marketplace Investments are rewarding. Business is very prosperous but you should be cautious of success and overabundance – don't overdo it. *Feng* advises against continuing with the same strategies (and products) that brought your enterprise to this state of prosperity; they will soon be outmoded and your enterprise must change with the times to keep up. *Feng* advises that old 'things' will be seen in a new and most favourable light. A possible example of this is the way women's fashions from the 1920s came back into vogue as mini skirts in the 1960s.

Telescopes and astronomy figure strongly in *Feng*.

Miscellaneous In the time of *Feng*, midday or noon is a particularly important part of day.

56 Lu 旅

Lu means travel, sojourn, stay away from home; self-sown; a stranger, a traveller, brigade, troops, force, together. Lu's components are **Fang**: a square, region, quarter, direction, recipe, plan, or way; correct, regular, just, then, now; **Shih**: clan or family; and the **radical** used in words concerning movement.

Image A traveller, a wanderer, a guest, an exile or a stranger in a strange land should be clear-minded, cautious and never in trouble with the local authorities.

In the field The farmer is going on a pilgrimage to a temple on a mountain. Before departure, the farmer makes offerings to all the realms of the spirit world, God, Heaven, and the ancestors, seeking blessings for a safe and successful journey.

Flow There is movement away from a situation with unstable foundations. Being in a new or unusual environment. You may go travelling soon or a traveller will come to your home.

All matters should be handled with clarity; quickly and effectively.

Lu suggests that penalties and lawsuits should be quick matters and not be dragged on indefinitely. Do not delay litigation if it is necessary. If there must be punishments or reprimands, let them be dealt with quickly. After that, do not dwell on the matter – move on with the journey of life.

Wealth You will certainly find the essential wealth needed. At this time there could be more wealth going out than coming in, so be cautious and prudent with resources. The illumination gained at this time has the potential for increasing all types of wealth further along your life path.

Relationships A stranger and guest in a strange land should stay only in proper places. Follow the customs of the area, but do not meddle in other people's politics, business or affairs. Do not give yourself airs. Be reserved and modest.

Good manners will benefit you. Do not flash your cash. Find honest helpers.

It is not a good time to form any sort of new union or partnership. People already planning to marry may change their minds. Work commitments may temporarily separate married couples.

Travel *Lu* advises on the prerequisites of good, safe travel. Whilst preparing for and beginning a journey, do not waste time with trivial or petty things or you may not get away at all. There are many essential things to be done, such as organising a seat or ticket on your mode of transport. These days, depending on the destination, passports, visas, innoculations and paperwork may also be required. Money is definitely needed. This is not the time for small-minded people, petty matters or vagueness. Clarity of thought is essential.

Those who travel for business reasons will experience good fortune.

Marketplace The travel industry and related enterprises make a fortune.

Employed people have more responsibility and prestige.

Women find worthwhile careers.

Scholars pass exams and find good jobs.

Fire should be watched and electrical equipment checked for faults.

Miscellaneous Lillia consulted the Insights about her prospects for the next three months and *Lu* was the answer. She could not see how she could go travelling, she had no plans to go travelling, certainly not enough money, and who would take care of her café if she went travelling anyway. Within a couple of weeks, it came about that her elderly mother-in-law had to take a trip to Greece and could not go by herself. There was a family meeting and it was decided Lillia should accompany the mother-in-law. The whole clan chipped in for her fare and expenses. Her sister-in-law looked after the café and Lillia went to Greece for a month.

57 Sun 巽

Sun means mild; peaceful. Its components, **Chi**: I; myself; self, private; personal, selfish; **Kung**: share; participate, all, altogether, collectively, wholly, totally; and **Hua**: plants, herbs, flowers. I share plants, herbs and flowers.

Image *Sun* is the place of wood, wind, air and sacred speech; words. Air penetrates the lungs. The roots of a tree penetrate the earth. The branches of a tree penetrate the sky recycling the air we breathe. Every time we breathe we create a wind. The wind penetrates every nook and cranny of the heavens. Knowledge and prosperity are carried by the wind wherever it blows. Listen to the sounds carried by the wind before movement is undertaken.

In the field There are dragon formations in the clouds and snakes in the grass and trees. The Tree of Life and Knowledge grows here, complete with Snake. *Kundalini* energy is ready and waiting to rise. Magicians and shamen are seen. Buddha is born, and lives and dies. The Goddess of Wealth and the Goddess of Learning appear. Kuan Yu, God of War and Protector against Evil and the Ravages of War, arrives.

Flow In the time of *Sun* all things develop and grow into the shape subsumed in their seed. It is time for completing projects. Make directives, instructions and commands known. Get on with undertakings and affairs. Success comes when the matter enquired about is quietly and persistently pursued in small steps.

Try to penetrate the meaning of a situation that is somehow hidden, then make a decision about the matter and act on it.

The beginning of your endeavours should be soft and gentle with three days of gradual and inconspicuous effects that bring success on the fourth day when a new direction or path can be found and taken. Continue faithfully in the new direction for three days after the new path is taken. This seven-day procedure creates an enduring activity that is lucky and prosperous.

Things that have been stuck or obstructed become free again.

Small things bring success. Veils and walls of illusion fall away.

Wealth There is nourishment and a good supply of wealth in and on all levels of your being. To have a goal or purpose is beneficial. Use the powers of the mind. Meditate and concentrate repeatedly on what is to be achieved. This is the way to put things in order.

Relationships Seek advice from a person who is very knowledgeable about the subject enquired about. Deep understanding and prosperity also come after a wise woman is consulted.

At this time, directives or instructions given to others need to be repeatedly given in order for those instructions to be clearly understood and acted upon.

Flexibility will make for harmonious working relationships.

Travel People will prosper in another land.

Good for the travel business and business that takes you travelling.

Marketplace There is three-fold gain in the marketplace. Wood products benefit.

Whether doing, making, buying, selling, or whatever, make it small for success. Small objects benefit.

Orators and wordsmiths benefit at this time.

Communications and communication technology benefit.

Judges act with clarity; they are fearless and outspoken.

Clear out clutter, old stuff and dust from under beds and the back of cupboards.

Miscellaneous Clear all channels, internal and external.

58 Dui 兑

Dui means barter, exchange, give an equivalent. Its components are **Hsiung**: an elder brother, a sensor; the **radical** for man's legs; and **K'ou**: mouth, entrance, pass.

Image Pleasure. Double joy. Success. Lake, marsh, rice paddy. Clouds. Clouds over the lake. An Insight lake that speaks.

In the field The harvest is in and the moon shines at its brightest. From planting time through the monsoon season, to harvesting and crop sales at the market, the peasants have toiled. Now they relax and celebrate a respite from work, enjoying the Autumn Harvest Festival. They barter and exchange products with one another. The peasants are pleased that they have some money and supplies but these resources must last until the next crop is harvested.

Flow At *Tui*'s finest there is *prema* – pure love that brings bliss. At *Tui*'s lowest there are indulgent pleasures that lead to battles and fighting.

Repair and prepare your defences, environments and resources; work while you are able to; this beneficial time will not last forever. Conditions change and things are not so easily fixed. Don't miss the opportunity offered.

Now is a good time to analyse and/or judge the work done, or actions taken, in the last year or that have brought your endeavours to this point. Positive thinking benefits.

Wealth You achieve success and receive benefits. In spiritual matters, there is a glimpse of *nitanandamayee* – eternal bliss.

Relationships Join with friends for discussion, activities and good times, but excessive talking can lead to trouble and loss of energy. So can too much food or the wrong type of food. The mouth and the stomach can both be a source of concern at this time if moderation and tact are not employed.

The mood is relaxed – you tend to view the world through rose-coloured glasses. Perhaps some of the good qualities you think you see in people and things at this time do not really exist – you could be easily led astray. Be light; be bright; but don't tell too much about yourself or your beliefs.

In love affairs, two women are involved with one man – both women should drop this guy like a hot potato. Married couples argue a lot.

Travel for business is very profitable. Travel for pleasure is pleasant (unless you are half of the married couple that is arguing a lot).

Marketplace It is a busy and prosperous marketplace. There is success in business – gold from the harvest. Business analysis and/or annual reports are a good idea at this time as they give a clear picture of where your business is heading and what will benefit it in the coming season.

Products used in winter or cold weather will sell well at this time.

A career in speaking, as a singer, actor, teacher, commentator or diplomat enjoys good fortune.

The unemployed will find work without effort.

Entertainment venues will prosper.

Feng shui *Dui* is marshy, swampy land with bad drainage; not the place to build a structure. Ideally, low-lying marshland and ponds should be situated to the west of any structures. Treasure may be found in such places in western areas. This treasure usually has something to do with water supply and/or irrigation.

Miscellaneous All shades of the colour pink, white or silver enhance your endeavours at this time, as do the colours of autumn and the sunset.

59 Huan 涣

Huan means disperse, scatter, melt, vanish. Components are **Shui**: water; and **Huan**: exchange, abundant, bright-coloured. Abundance moving over water.

Image The wind propels a piece of wood that is floating on the water.

In the field The ancients say that it was *Huan*'s image and the realisation that wood floats on water that caused people to scoop out tree trunks for boats and harden wood in the fire to make oars. Once they had the boats, trade, communications and migration followed. Some of the best ideas for recovery or expansion are based on simple observation.

Flow The prophecy is good. It's time for action. It's time to expand. *Huan* is all about change. The time is perfect for a change or movement of some kind.

Change your attitudes or ideas. Change your troubles to good fortune. Venture into new territory for gains, for protection and insight.

Huan is all about using innovative ideas and action to solve problems. In order to scatter, disperse or indeed vanish, 'things' in your life will have to be broken up.

Certain problems that arise at this time can be resolved by taking positive action and seeking assistance from people or institutes that support your endeavours.

There is a great idea in the offering; it becomes the central point for the organisation of recovery. Effort will be required to turn this great idea into something tangible.

Wealth Some type of property will be sold, given away or dispersed of in one way or another. Sometimes you should give up something for much less than it is worth. Doing this will enable you to accomplish something that will lead to a lot more wealth than you began with. Small-thinking people don't trust or believe this concept.

Relationships Capable people come and help. From the beginning, be clear to these people as to your intentions. This will reduce the possibility of misunderstandings later.

If you begin to think badly about others and are generally in a bad mood, *Huan* says look within yourself for the source of the problem. The way of the *Dao* is to stop in a quiet place and do some deep breathing. Relaxation exercises or meditation will benefit you greatly.

A relative has the answer you seek.

A separation in the family is temporary.

At this time, you or the person enquired about will be too busy to get married.

Travel If you truly need to travel far away, perhaps taking only your nearest and dearest; go for it, it is the right thing to do. There is good fortune in travelling to another place for an undertaking. It is a good time to move your home.

Marketplace Change brings prosperity.

Change your career.

Begin a new project.

Open a new branch of your business.

Exchange and trade across water; the marketplace across the water.

A *feng* (wind) *shui* (water) consultation benefits.

Miscellaneous Andrew, who lived in Auckland, was offered a very good job in Sydney. But he would have to be in Sydney in one month with his wife and three children in order to start the job. He consulted the Insights about whether he should take the job and uproot the family and how he would pay for the venture. *Huan* was the answer. After a family conference they decided unanimously to do it. They had a very big and very successful garage sale. Andrew sold his car and some paintings for much less than they were worth, and they scraped together enough money. This was seven years ago and now Andrew and his family are well established, prosperous and happy in Sydney.

60 Jie 節

Jie means regulate, restrict, limit, standardise, economise; knot, joint, section, a length. **Jie's** components are **Ji**: approach, reach, be near, at present; and **Zhu**: bamboo. The regular distances between the joints in bamboo were used for all types of measuring and made into flutes and pitch pipes to create standard tones and sounds in music.

Image By making regulations and understanding limitations and using both to advantage, misery can be transformed into happiness. Set limits on expenditures and actions, but harsh or severe regulations will never succeed.

In the field *Jie* pictures the time from autumn to after the winter solstice when movement and renewal of resources was limited. Regulations and limitations needed to be imposed for supplies to last. Fortunately, the seasons are also regulated and the farmer knows that limitations of winter will disappear in the spring.

Flow At first there are conditions that limit any activities that take you outside your front door. Accept these limitations and remain still; gathering energy to overcome these limitations will bring good fortune. Coming to a stop. You are strong but should limit actions to avoid pitfalls at this time. Go with the flow; use regulations and limitations to your advantage; it will give you time to work out many matters. The right moment to go forth will arrive and you will know it.

When the time of limitations passes (and it will, just as surely as the spring will arrive), do not try to maintain the same restrictions and limitations, it is time to go forth. Limitation has brought you to inner truth and your light needs limitations no longer.

Wealth Do not be afraid to share your resources at this time. Sometimes you may go over the limit, exhausting energy and resources, you and will have good reason to berate yourself severely in the aftermath. Because you learn your lesson, the universe is kind and provides more energy and resources. You should faithfully set limits on these new resources that you can abide by.

If resources are used well, you can be very content living or working in limited circumstances. This will leave your mind and time free for creative thought and endeavours, then your reputation will grow.

Relationships Set limits on yourself first. Make these limits reasonable and sweet, then others will follow your example; this will bring good fortune. Play your role exactly as the job description states it should be played; the limits of duty or *dharma* (right action). Keep to the middle way; avoid extremes; keep a good sense of proportion.

Harsh, severe or unsuitable restrictions won't succeed. If something or someone has to be limited, confined or restricted, this should be done in such a way that the restrictions are in harmony with the restricted thing or person's nature, for example, a duck should be confined near water. *Jie* says restrictions should be applied in such a way that growth and development of those restricted will not be stunted.

There is good news from those far away.

Marketplace In business avoid large expenses but be ready when opportunity beckons.

Industries or enterprises involved with measurements, regulations or the standardisation of something will prosper.

Feng shui If you have asked about premises or land, the prognosis is not good. The ground is waterlogged and marshy.

61 Zhong Fu 中孚

Together, the characters **Zhong Fu** mean inner truth or confidence. **Zhong** means middle, centre, inner, inside. **Fu** means trust, having confidence, inspiring confidence. **Fu**'s components are **Zi**: young, small egg, seed, children, students; and **Zhao**: talons, legs, an ancient title of respect for a learned or virtuous person.

Image When inner sincerity and confidence produce inspiration and trust, people are transformed and united by it. Then great deeds can be done successfully.

In the field The crops are growing towards perfection. The seedlings are now healthy plants but they still have to grow some more before harvesting. The farmer is still irrigating, tending and weeding. Cranes call to one another across the fields. The wind penetrates the mist or haze over the lake and carries sound across it; communications.

Flow When beginning your endeavours, stay calm. If possible, stay by yourself and definitely keep your own counsel and maintain inner confidence. Be vigilant; prepare, think and worry. Do all sorts of predictions from business and growth forecasts through to divining with *I Ching* yarrow or coins.

This is the time to take a new direction alone if your endeavours require more choices and autonomy. Cheerful good manners aid your new course.

An increase in resources or wealth of some kind puts you in a glorious mood and a friend comes unexpectedly to share your joy. When you speak sincerely at this time, your words are picked up as thoughts far away. Just as wind carries sound across a lake, words spoken for good or bad at this time penetrate nooks and crannies far away and people are subtly influenced. So think positive thoughts.

However words are not enough. Deeds that mirror the words must be done and be seen to be done. Show restraint when success comes – overconfidence and alcohol are detrimental.

Wealth increases in all realms of your being.

The flow of *chi* created by *Zhong Fu* increases clear thinking and energy levels. Don't lose focus and concentration. Keep a strong hold on the senses and desires.

Relationships People are attracted by your sincerity, gentleness and love. The force of your inner truth grows so great that you can influence all types of people and creatures effortlessly.

Observe the omens in your environment by noting the movements and behaviour of the people sharing that environment.

A person who relies on another for strength and stability is tossed on the ocean of life, up and down, according to the other's whim. For success you must find strength, stability and confidence within yourself.

When dealing with others' mistakes or crimes, try to stand in their shoes and understand their motivations. Consider the reason why the mistake or crime took place as well as the mistake or crime itself. Go to the core of the problem and fix that. Secret agendas don't benefit. Avoid biased people.

Family and friends cooperate. It is a good time for love and marriage. Blessings of children and fertility will come. A successful celebration, party, convention, or religious ceremony occurs.

Travel Journeys by or over water are advantageous.

Marketplace The north-east direction in the southern hemisphere or the south-east in the northern hemisphere benefits. As well as being actual directions, these areas symbolise a place where things are in production or are produced for the marketplace, a place where people work towards their goals, a place where people communicate.

Activity and business in the marketplace is growing at a very healthy rate and it hasn't peaked yet. There is a great market for your product.

62 Xiao Guo 小過

Xiao means small. **Guo** means cross, pass by, pass time, over, go beyond, through or over, undergo a process; unduly excessive; fault, mistake.

Image Great good fortune comes if you can exceed ordinary standards in, or through, the use and care of small things.

In the field It is early spring and young green shoots are popping up all over the mountain. The farmer takes care of little things; the sowing of seeds and the gentle tending of small seedlings. The weather and conditions are not right for big things yet.

Flow The time is right for small things such as new ideas, endeavours or projects that have just germinated or come to light. Big things have no success right now. Flying too high and attempting great feats or endeavours at this time has unfortunate consequences. Call a halt to any flashy, attention-seeking behaviour. Stick to the usual ways, and ordinary things and activities. If there is something dangerous, risky, nerve-racking or scary that must be done, do it quickly.

Wealth Things are not perfect but soon they will improve if excessive attention is paid to all the small details in everything that is done.

Be frugal. Consider economy as the greatest of virtues and watch every penny. You will get the money you need.

Relationships In keeping with the time, meet with minor officials and officers rather than highly placed people. Generally speaking, women will be of more help to you than men at this time.

You could be caught in the middle, between two factions or two people with very different opinions about an issue. You would like to see both sides make peace. Others might not agree with your views; they can become hostile and 'hit' you from behind. It is best to keep a low profile for now. Times will change and your enthusiasm will find support and helpers. Only open-minded, intuitive people will be receptive to your ideas right now.

Sometimes a problem cannot be avoided. It stands directly in your path and needs to be removed before any other movement is possible – so you cannot get around it. Helpers are needed to overcome this problem, but you need the right helpers. The helpers needed are not well known, you must seek them out. Stay with the ordinary, everyday people and act simply to achieve success.

A person that you love may physically disappear from your life but the love you share with this person will never disappear.

Travel Air travel at this time is not recommended but land or water is alright.

Marketplace In business and the corporate sector, small objects, deals, and 'things' bring the best returns.

Pay close attention to contract details. Conclude business and trade quickly.

Upstairs premises are not the place for the enquirer or the person enquired about at this time; downstairs premises or single-storey buildings will benefit you.

Feng shui The premises or room enquired about contains a 'door to the spirit world'; it is the 'mysterious place of endings and beginnings' and is not a good place to live or sleep. It is OK for daylight or busy, noisy business premises, and good for temples and religious practices.

If you do live or sleep in this building, room or area, place a symbolic guardian in this area and orientate it towards the south-east in the southern hemisphere or north-east in the northern hemisphere. This symbolic guardian should be an entity that suits you; someone or something you consider as a powerful protective force. This guardian could be represented by a painting, photo or statue.

63 Ji Ji 既濟

Ji means already, since, done with, finished. **Ji** means completion, accomplishment; cross a river, relieve.

Image Something is achieved successfully. After completion is not the end. The wheel keeps turning. *Ji Ji* shows the way to maintain the momentum and energy that has brought you this far.

In the field The crop has been harvested but the farmer can't rest yet. There are many small jobs that still have to be done before winter.

Flow Everything seems to be in perfect order. Unless this order is maintained constantly and vigorously, it will become the beginning of disorder. Everything seems to proceed of its own accord. You are tempted to relax and let things take their course without troubling over detail. This is wrong – decay will creep in. Attend to all small details and things vigilantly, settle matters quickly as they arise and stay up-to-date; don't let things build up. Perseverance, timely precautions and planning foresight are the way to success. After completing one thing, don't immediately rush into something new; think carefully first.

Your endeavours may take you into new and sometimes hostile territory that will take some time and energy to develop. There is a fair amount of confusion and disorder to sort out. Use the services of capable people, who are knowledgeable about conditions in the new territory.

It will be a-one-step-forward-and-three-steps-backwards kind of time. The closer you come to your goal, the more distractions appear. Stay focused.

Wealth The biggest and brightest is not necessarily the best. Simple, genuine sentiment expressed from the heart receives the blessing, then you will have success. This is an excellent time for all types of small things.

If something has been lost, it will return within seven days. What truly belongs to you, be it idea or object, will always belong to you and cannot be lost. Do not seek ways to draw attention to yourself. Waiting brings blessings; the *Daoist* way of action through non-action.

Relationships There are impediments to the route others are taking around you. Don't be caught up in their enthusiasm. Be your own person, concerned totally with your own affairs. Consider options and resources, try lateral thinking.

When you have succeeded in your independent endeavour, try not to make your success the centre of attention as it will make others jealous and obstructive. Just keep quietly moving forward without looking back. Celebrating success by getting drunk will be unfortunate.

Missing persons return.

Married couples experience peace and harmony. Lovers should marry soon.

Travel by water or travel for pleasure is not recommended at this time

It is not a good idea to move your house or home for any reason at this time. Even though this move may seem a sound idea and those around you may be in favour of it, this move will not be to your advantage.

Marketplace Maintain the present state of business – do not expand.

Unexpected problems arise that need to be attended to properly for ultimate success. Because of the pace of activities at this time, there is a tendency to fix problems quickly with short-term solutions that must be constantly checked and reinforced. Fix the problem properly or your endeavour may sink.

You are likely to be promoted at work.

It is a time for top marks and recognition for students, scholars and academics.

Don't get in over your head.

Miscellaneous You find what you are looking for.

64 Wei Ji 未濟

Together, the characters **Wei Ji** mean have not completed. **Wei** means have not, did not, no. **Wei**'s ancient character pictures a tree with fully grown branches. **Ji** means completion, accomplishment, crossing a river; relieve, ferry.

Image You know exactly what needs to be done; but you haven't done it yet.

In the field Sunshine and new endeavours. The growing season begins again and farmers get ready to plant new crops. The farmer has decided what to plant and where it is to be planted, the right seed has been selected and any equipment needed is standing by. The farmer has planned exactly what has to be done. Now all the farmer has to do is the actual work.

Flow *Wei Ji* pictures the transition from an ending of one situation to establishing a new one.

At the beginning, vision is hazy and things aren't seen clearly. It is best to hold back and contemplate your moves. Gather enough energy to carry you through this time of transition to a new and better time. There's a lot of hard work ahead. When you do begin to act, move slowly, almost in slow motion and take thought at every step.

Get help to overcome any immediate obstacles and do things that must be done, but don't advance any further than completely necessary. A flash of creative genius (a very good idea) will provide you with the next successful step forward.

But there is still some hard work to do and discipline is needed, as there is something of a battle to overcome internal and external hostilities to your endeavours. In *Wei Ji* there is a lot of learning and teaching and falling over your feet, but what you accomplish at this time is the basis of a successful new situation.

Wealth New activities to create wealth in any level of your being will be extremely successful. Your light is true and your clarity, intuition, intelligence and inner sincerity bring success. The new situation will be so much better than the old – that is a wondrous thing!

Put everything in its proper place for increased prosperity; consult a feng shui practitioner if necessary.

At first, money is a source of anxiety. If you are waiting for money to arrive it might be delayed, but people will help. New investments will prosper in the long term.

Relationships Success often attracts some sneaky people; compromise with them rather than become embroiled in a (legal) conflict.

After such an industrious and successful time, it is good and wise to gather with friends, helpers and supporters. But getting intoxicated isn't a good idea; it could undermine some of the good work done.

Men should defer to women's opinions. Women at this time have a better understanding of the situation and see things more clearly.

All kinds of new partnerships should be considered carefully and perhaps deferred for at least a month.

Travel If travel is part of your movement towards a new situation, it will take a great burden from your shoulders. However, organising it may take patience and a cool head.

Marketplace Is there some unfinished project or business you should be doing? Then hurry and finish it! New enterprises will also be successful. After the new enterprise is established, don't expand activities any further. Maintain present conditions and pay extra attention to detail.

If you live above ground floor level, beware of burglars in the night.

Miscellaneous The way of Dao is endless; at the end there is a new beginning.

On this hopeful note of new creative movement, the I Ching returns to *#1 Qian*.

Acknowledgements

Thank you, thank you, thank you!

To Neville Whitehead for his loving patience, encouragement and support. To Wilson Lawler and Seth Lawler for providing me with an opportunity to understand selfless service and to view the world through their eyes. To Elizabeth Horsbough for being the best friend anyone could ever hope to have. To Julie Stanton at Simon & Schuster for always having confidence in my abilities. To Clare Wallis for gently and patiently taking me through the final editing processes of this book.

To Richard Wilhelm, Dr Wen Kuan Chu, Wallace A. Sherrill, Wu Jing Nuan, Da Lui, Derek Walters, and Jean-Michael Huon de Kermadec for all their scholarly research and work that has made my work possible. Even though several of these gentleman departed this earth many years ago, through their writings they have become my mentors and friends. Many times in the last 17 years as I worked away, late into the night, I would not have been the least surprised to turn around and see Richard Wilhelm, Dr Chu or Mr Sherrill leaning over my shoulder reading my work.

Very special thanks to Sri Satya Sai Baba for waking me up and giving me insight, direction and faith.

Bibliography

I Ching

Chu, W. K. and Sherrill, W. A. 1976, *The Anthology of I Ching*, Routledge & Kegan Paul, London.

Chu, W. K. and Sherrill, W. A. 1985, *The Astrology of I Ching*, Routledge & Kegan Paul, London.

Da Liu 1975, *I Ching Coin Prediction*, Routledge & Kegan Paul, London.

Damien-Knight, Guy 1987, *Karma and Destiny in the I Ching*, Routledge and Kegan Paul, New York.

Dhiegh, Khigh Aix 1978, *I Ching: Taoist Book of Days Calendar-Diary 1979*, Ballentine Books, New York.

Dhiegh, Khigh Aix 1978, *I Ching: Taoist Book of Days Calendar-Diary 1980*, Ballentine Books, New York.

Dhiegh, Khigh Aix 1978, *I Ching: Taoist Book of Days Calendar-Diary 1982*, Ballentine Books, New York.

Ffarington Hook, D. *The I Ching and its Associations*, Routledge & Kegan Paul, London. Out of print.

Ffarington Hook, D. *The I Ching and Mankind*, Routledge & Kegan Paul, London. Out of print.

Ffarington Hook, D. *The I Ching and You*, Routledge & Kegan Paul, London. Out of print.

Huon de Kermadec, Jean-Michel, *Heavenly Pennies*, Poulsen, Derek (trans.), Mandala Books (Unwin Paperbacks).

MacHovec, Frank J. 1971, *I Ching (The Book of Changes)*, Peter Pauper Press Inc., New York.

Reifler, Sam, 1974, *I Ching*, Bantam Books, Toronto.

Waltham, Clae 1969, *I Ching – The Chinese Book of Changes*, arranged from the work of James Legge, Ace Publishing Corporation, New York.

Wilhelm, Hellmut 1975, *Change – Eight Lectures on the I Ching*, Baynes, Cary F. (trans.), Routledge & Kegan Paul, London.

Wilhelm, Richard 1975, *The I Ching or Book of Change*, 3rd edn, Baynes, Cary F. (trans.), Routledge & Kegan Paul, London.

Wu Jing-Nuan 1991, *Yi Jing*, The Taoist Centre, Washington DC.

Mythology

Translators Yang X, Yang G and others 1983, *Ancient Chinese Fables*, Foreign Languages Press, Beijing.

Chin, Lucie M. 1990, *The Fairy of Ku She*, Fontana/Collins, UK.

Christie, Anthony, 1983, *Chinese Mythology*, Chancellor, London.

Latach, M. 1984 *Chinese Traditional Festivals*, New World Press, Beijing.

Muller, F. Max 1965, *The Sacred Book of the East*, Motilal Banarsidass, Delhi.

Sanders, Tao Tao Li 1980, *Dragon, Gods and Spirits from Chinese Mythology*, Hodder & Stoughton, Sydney.

Wa, Cheng-en 1980, *The Pilgrimage to the West*, Seagull Publishing Co., Hong Kong.

Werner, Edward T. C. 1995, *Ancient Tales and Folklore of China*, Senate/Studio Editions Ltd, England

Dao

Lao, Tzu 1985, *Tao Te Ching*, Wilhelm, Richard (ed.), Ostwald, H. G. (trans), Arkana, London.

Li, Ju-chen 1965, *Flowers in the Mirror*, Lin Tai-yi (trans.), Peter Owen, London.

Wilhem, Richard 1962, *The Secret of the Golden Flower*, Harcourt Brace Jovanovich, New York.

Buddhism

Evans-Wentz, W.Y., 1971, *The Tibetan Book of the Dead*, Oxford University Press, New York.

Evans-Wentz, W. Y. 1969, *The Tibetan Book of the Great Liberation*, Oxford University Press, New York.

Govinda, Lama Anagarika 1982, *The Way of the White Clouds*, B. I. Publications, New Delhi.

Govinda, Lama Anagarika 1983, *Foundations of Tibetan Mysticism*, Rider, London. (This book also contains information on chakras.)

Humphreys, Christmas 1962,

Buddhism, Cassell, London.

Mascaro, Juan 1973, *The Dhammapada*, Penguin, Middlesex, England.

Other

Temple, R. 1987, *The Genius of China*, Simon and Schuster, New York.

Bush, Richard C. 1970, *Religion in Communist China*, Abingdon Press, Nashville.

Chang, Chi-yun 1975, *A Life of Confucius*, China Academy, Taipei.

Chung, Tsai Chih 1991, *The Sayings of Mencius: Wisdom in a Chaotic Era*, Ng En Tzu, Mary (trans.), Asiapac Books, Singapore.

Edwards, E. D. 1948, *Lotus, Bamboo and Palm*, William Hodge and Co. Ltd, UK.

Fawdry, Marguerite 1977, *Chinese Childhood*, Pollacks Toy Theatres Ltd, London.

Fong, Wen 1980, *The Great Bronze Age of China*, Thames and Hudson, London.

Gascoigne, Bamber 1973, *The Treasures and Dynasties of China*, Viking Press, New York.

Gernet, Jacques 1970, *Daily Life in China on the Eve of the Mongol Invasion 1250–1276*, Stanford University Press, California.

Hung-Chao, Tai 1989, *Confuciansim and Economic Development: An Oriental Alternative*, Washington Institute Press, Washington.

Jung, C. G. 1963, *Memories, Dreams, Reflections*, Jaffe, Anicia (ed.), Routledge & Kegan Paul, London.

Jung, C. G. 1933, *Modern Man in Search of a Soul*, Routledge & Kegan Paul, London.

Kedd, David 1960, *All the Emperor's Horses*, John Murray, London.

Legge, James 1891, *Books of the East*, Vol. 39–40, The Texts of Taoism, Graham Brash, Singapore.

Life Editorial Staff 1959, *The World's Great Religions*, Collins, London.

Lin, Yutang 1943, *The Wisdom of Confucius*, A. S. Barnes, New York.

Palmer, Martin 1986, *The Ancient Chinese Almanac*, Rider & Co., London, England.

Prodan, Mario 1966, *Intro to Chinese Art*, Sping Books, London.

Sinclair, Kevin 1987, *The Forgotten Tribes of China*, Child & Associates, Brookvale, NSW, Australia.

Tae, Hung Ha 1969, *Tales From the Three Kingdoms*, Yonsei University Press, Seoul.

Tham, Seong Chee 1985, *Religion and Modernization: A Study of Changing Rituals Among*

Singapore's Chinese, Malays and Indians, Graham Brash, Singapore.

Williams, C. A. S. 1960, *Encyclopedia of Chinese Symbolism and Art Motives*, The Julian Press, New York.

Feng Shui and Astrology

Carus, Paul 1974, *Chinese Astrology*, La Salle, Illinois.

Huon de Kermadec, Jean-Michel 1983, *The Way to Chinese Astrology: The Four Pillars of Destiny*, Poulsen, N. Derek (trans.), Unwin Paperbacks, Boston and Sydney.

Skinner, Stephen 1983, *The Living Earth Manual of Feng Shui*, Graham Brash (Pte) Ltd, Singapore.

Walters, Derek 1987, *Chinese Astrology*, The Aquarian Press, Northamptonshire, England.

Walters, Derek 1988, *Feng Shui*, Pagoda, UK.

Walters, Derek 1991, *The Feng Shui Handbook*, The Aquarian Press, London.